MODELS OF BUSINESS CYCLES

Yrjö Waldemar Jahnsson, 1877–1936, was Professor of Economics at the Institute of Technology, Helsinki. In 1954, his wife Hilma Jahnsson established, in accordance with her husband's wishes, a foundation. The specific purpose of the Yrjö Jahnsson Foundation is to promote economic research in Finland. To this end the Foundation supports the work of individual scholars and institutions by awarding them scholarships and grants. It also invites internationally renowned economists to Finland to give courses of lectures which are then published in this series.

YRJÖ JAHNSSON LECTURES

Models of Business Cycles

Robert E. Lucas Jr

Basil Blackwell

Copyright © Yrjö Jahnsson Foundation 1987

First published 1987
Reprinted 1990
First published in paperback 1988
Reprinted 1990

Basil Blackwell Ltd
108 Cowley Road, Oxford OX4 1JF, UK

Basil Blackwell, Inc.
3 Cambridge Center
Cambridge, Massachusetts 02142, USA

British Library Cataloguing in Publication Data
A CIP catalogue record for this book is available from
the British Library.

Library of Congress Cataloging in Publication Data
Lucas, Robert E.
Models of business cycles.

(Yrjö Jahnsson lectures)
Bibliography:p.
Includes index.
1. Business cycles – Mathematical models. I. Title.
II. Series.
HB3711.L82   1987   338.5'42'0724   86-17622
ISBN 0–631–14789–6
ISBN 0–631–14791–8 (pbk.)

Typeset by Unicus Graphics Ltd, Horsham

Contents

Preface

This book consists of the Yrjö Jahnsson Lectures that I gave in Helsinki in May 1985. The visit to Finland was a pleasure as well as an honor, thanks to the warm hospitality shown to Nancy Stokey and me by Seppo and Sirkku Honkapohja and many other Finnish friends.

Nancy Stokey and Laurence Weiss read the manuscript before the lectures were given, and their suggestions led to many improvements. Robert Tamura assisted me in assembling references. June Nason efficiently typed several drafts of the lectures, and then the final version that appears here. My thanks to each of them, and also to the National Science Foundation and the Yrjö Jahnsson Foundation for their support.

To my father

I

Research in my field of specialization – macroeconomics, or monetary and business cycle
theory – has undergone rapid change in the past
15 years. One way of describing some of these
changes is in terms of ideological contests between
rival schools of thought: the 'Keynesian revolution', the 'monetarist counter-revolution', and so
on. There is no doubt something to be learned by
tracing the main ideological currents in macroeconomic research, but I myself find most of this
discussion of crises, revolutions and so on, unintel-
ligible, and almost wholly unconnected with the
most interesting current research. Recent macroeconomic controversy seems to me much more
easily interpreted as a surface manifestation of
much deeper and more important developments in
economic theory, developments that long predate
current macroeconomic controversies and that
will be of importance long after these controversies have gone the way of the liquidity trap, opera-
tion twist, the loanable funds doctrine, and all the

[1]

other macroeconomic issues that seemed so important as they were occurring and are so hard to remember now.

Dynamic economic theory – I mean theory in the sense of models that one can write down and *do* something with, not in the sense of 'opinion' or 'belief' – has simply been reinvented in the last 40 years. It is now entirely routine to analyze economic decision-makers as operating through time in a complex, probabilistic environment, trading in a rich array of contingent-claim securities, and to study agents situated in economies with a wide variety of possible technologies, information structures, and stochastic disturbances. While Keynes and the other founders of what we now call macroeconomics were obliged to rely on Marshallian ingenuity to tease some useful dynamics out of purely static theory, the modern theorist is much better equipped to state *exactly* the problem he wants to study and then to study it.

This new ability to incorporate dynamic and probabilistic elements into economic theory, at the same level of rigor on which we study the problem of a single decision-maker making a one-time choice at given prices, has already had a deep, permanent influence on virtually every branch of applied economics. What people refer to as the 'rational expectations revolution' in macroeconomics is mainly the manifestation, in one field of application, of a development that is affecting *all* fields of application. To try to understand and

[2]

explain these events as though they were primarily a reaction to Keynes and Keynesianism is futile. One may as well try to understand parallel developments in industrial organization as a reaction to Viner or Chamberlain or in public finance as a reaction to Pigou or Musgrave.

In macroeconomics, certainly, this process of dynamicization is very far from completed, and I do not believe it has yet taken us to a satisfactory theoretical account of the events we group together under the term 'business cycle'. Yet even at this early stage, I think it is evident that certain habits of thought that are central to the way we have thought about macroeconomics and macroeconomic policy since the Second World War need to be replaced with a point of view that is in some ways radically different.

I would like to use these lectures as an opportunity to describe some of these developments, and the changes in viewpoint they seem to me to necessitate. I will begin, in section II, by discussing some general considerations that seem to me to be important in deciding which kinds of economic models might permit us to determine the effects that economic policies will have on people's consumption streams and welfare. Section III confronts a hypothetical consumer, in an experimental spirit, with some different consumption paths, and traces out his reactions to them, in an attempt to get a quantitative idea of the importance of stabilization policy relative to other economic questions.

[3]

Section IV moves to an exposition and discussion of a particular model of aggregate activity due to Finn Kydland and Edward Prescott. This model seems to me to offer a useful definition of the current frontier in business cycle research and I will use it as a point of departure in discussing outstanding questions.

Sections V and VI deal with two issues from which Kydland and Prescott abstract, but which many believe to be at the center of the problem of business cycles. Section V surveys certain aspects of the theory of unemployment. Section VI introduces monetary complications.

Section VII considers the prospects for a model of business cycles centered on the role of monetary disturbances. Though this is the subject, of all those considered in the lectures, to which I have devoted the most thought – and with good judgement, I continue to believe – it is also that on which the least is known and I will rely heavily on conjecture. I will sum up these matters in the last section.

When I began work on these lectures, I had in mind something like a broad and balanced survey of recent developments. Now that I am finished, it is easy enough to see the ways in which I have been guided by research prejudices that cannot (at least as yet!) be said to have been verified by hard results and also the ways in which I have been limited by the narrowness of my own technical range. In particular, I will not treat in any detail the econometric developments that I think may well be the most lasting contribution of John Muth's idea of rational expectations. A good introduction to these ideas is contained in a volume Thomas Sargent and I edited,[1] and to which Sargent is the leading contributor, but I will not be reviewing these developments here.

1 Robert E. Lucas, Jr and Thomas J. Sargent (eds), *Rational Expectations and Econometric Practice* (University of Minnesota Press, Minneapolis, 1981).

II

Discussions of economic policy, if they are to be productive in any practical sense, necessarily involve quantitative assessments of the way proposed policies are likely to affect resource allocation and individual welfare. This means that useful policy discussions are ultimately based on *models*, not in the sense that policy decisions can be automated once and for all without the need for individual judgements, but in the sense that participants in the discussion must have, explicitly or implicitly, some way of making a quantitative connection between policies and their consequences. I want to spend almost all of my time in these lectures, then, on issues involved in the construction of useful economic models. Although this will lead us into technical issues that seem far removed from current policy debates, I think this is ultimately the most – perhaps the *only* – practical way to proceed. Macroeconomics receives a great deal of attention in the newspapers, but this is not the level at which progress is made or continuity is to be discovered.

In a general way, the problem of macroeconomics – really, of *all* applied economics – is to go from non-experimental observations on the past behavior of the economy to inferences about the future behavior of the economy under alternative assumptions about the way policy is conducted. In terms of models, then, we want a model that fits historical data and that can be simulated to give reliable estimates of the effects of various policies on future behavior. But *what* data? And what do we mean by *fit?* And when can we expect that particular simulations will be *reliable?* These are hard questions, harder and more open than is commonly acknowledged, and nothing is more dangerous than the illusion that they can be answered by 'common sense'. It will be helpful, I think, to consider these questions in a very general way before turning to the construction of specific, operational models.

A useful model, to begin at the very end of the story, is going to take the form of an explicit description of the way the economy evolves through time. We will want to consider stochastically disturbed systems, so let e_t denote independent drawings of an exogenous shock from some fixed distribution $G(e)$, and let the law of motion of s_t, a complete description of the 'state of the system' at date t, be denoted:

$$s_{t+1} = F(s_t, e_t).$$

Think of s_t as a vector with many components, including the economic variables of primary interest, such as the date t consumption of the agents in the system, underlying intermediate variables like stocks of capital goods and inventories, policy variables and perhaps variables of no intrinsic importance except that they contain information useful in forecasting future values of these other variables. Similarly, think of the shock vector e_t as a vector with many components.

We could think of proceeding empirically by identifying the state vector s_t with observable magnitudes and estimating F and G from economic data. This, very roughly, would give us what an econometrician would call a 'reduced form' description of the system. Such a description might be useful in forecasting future s_t values (this would depend on the stability of the estimated reduced form over time), and perhaps, as Christopher Sims and George Stigler have argued in different ways, this is all we can hope to do anyway.[1] But if, as I

1 I associate with Stigler (for example, George J. Stigler, *The Citizen and the State* (University of Chicago Press, Chicago, 1975)) and Sims (for example, Christopher A. Sims, 'Policy analysis with econometric models', *Brookings Papers on Economic Activity* (1982), pp. 107–64) the view of social science as most usefully standing outside the political as well as the economic system, attempting to forecast and understand the behavior of both without attempting to influence either. The normative, welfare–economic tradition is, in contrast, unabashedly utopian, treating the behavior of the private sector as something to be predicted, and that of the public sector as something to be reformed. Stigler, with some justice, calls this a 'deeply schizophrenic view of the state'.

have been taking for granted and will continue to do, our objective is to determine how *changes* in those aspects of the system we call 'policies' induce *changes* in individual consumption and welfare, we need much more knowledge about F and G than simply the forms that fit certain historical data.

The problem, of course, is that the motion F of an economic system depends, in a very complicated way, not only on actions we would want to call 'policies' but on the actions of all of the agents that make up the system. At an abstract level, we can say that a policy change involves a shift from one law F to another, F' say, but operationally, we have no direct way of knowing how particular policy changes translate into F-changes.

We can move toward what an econometrician would call a 'structural' description of the system, by refining the specification of F so as to differentiate between actions taken by private agents and those taken by 'nature' (including in the latter term 'policies'). To set up a notation that reflects this

---

Sims criticizes the 'rational expectations revolution' for 'destroying or discarding much that was valuable in the name of utopian ideology'. See Thomas J. Sargent, 'Autoregressions, expectations and advice', *American Economic Review* **74** (1984), pp. 408–15, for a useful discussion of Sim's position.

There is no point in arguing over which of these positions is correct; the answer must be 'neither' or 'both'. Throughout these lectures, I will be consistently taking the schizophrenic, utopian point of view.

distinction, let 'nature' take action $z_t = z(s_t)$ when the state of the economy is s_t, and let agent i take action $a_{it} = a_i(s_t)$, with $a_t = a(s_t)$ denoting the vector of *all* actions taken by all agents. Then if $s_{t+1} = H(z_t, a_t, s_t, e_t)$ when the shock is e_t and nature and private agents take the actions (z_t, a_t), we can express F as

$$F(s_t, e_t) = H(z(s_t), a(s_t), s_t, e_t).$$

Is this translation progress? This depends on whether the changes in policy we want to analyze are easily translated into changes in the way we specify the function $z(\cdot)$ (describing 'nature's' actions) *and* if we have reason to believe that the functions $H(\cdot)$ and $a(\cdot)$ do not vary in responses to these changes in policy $z(\cdot)$. This is exactly the case for 'structural' estimation (estimation of H, a and z separately) as opposed to 'reduced form' estimation that Marschak made in his classic Cowles paper: if policy shifts the supply function in a known way, and if it does not shift the demand function, then knowing demand and supply parameters separately permits us to predict the price and quantity effects of the policy, while knowing only the reduced form does not.[2]

---

2 Jacob Marschak, 'Economic measurements for policy and prediction', in William C. Hood and Tjalling G. Koopmans (eds), *Studies in Econometric Method*, Cowles Commission Monograph 14 (Wiley, New York, 1953), pp. 1–26.

There are interesting problems in economics for which this is as far as one needs to go, but the issues in economic dynamics that arise in macroeconomics are not among them. The problem, as is now widely recognized, is that there is no reason to expect that the function $a(\cdot)$ describing agents' actions will remain invariant under changes in the function $z(\cdot)$ describing nature's actions. If agents are interested in maximizing an objective function, say the expected utility from the stochastic consumption streams they receive, they will choose actions a_{it} in order to try to achieve this objective. I have not as yet spelled out the decision problem faced by these agents in a way that would permit us to see exactly what function or 'decision rule' will achieve this, but it is clear enough simply from the facts that the agents are interested in their future consumption and are operating in a changing environment that one would expect their decision rules $a_i(\cdot)$ to adapt in response to changes in policy $z(\cdot)$. To imagine otherwise is to assume that the solution to a maximum problem does not vary with changes in the function being maximized! Given this, the identification of the 'structure' in the sense of the functions H, a and z gives us no more ability to determine the consequences of policy changes than does knowledge of the 'reduced form' F. We need a deeper idea of what we mean by 'structure', not because 'depth' is desirable in itself – a key to success in applied science, I think, it to operate on as shallow a level as one can get by with – but

[11]

because a model has to be able to isolate those aspects of behavior that remain invariant to policy shifts from those that do not if it is to be of any use in assessing the consequences of the shift.[3]

It will clarify what I mean by a 'useful structure' to set out some additional formalism, though I must say in advance that the formalism I will write down is both too general to do anything with, analytically, and also too 'special' in the sense that it is easy to think of interesting dynamic models that it does not subsume as special cases. Let us imagine that at a given date, when the system is in state s, nature selects an action z and each agent i selects an action a_i from an opportunity set $\Omega_i(a_{-i}, s, z)$ that is determined by the state s, nature's action z, and the actions a_{-i} taken by all other agents. Denote the immediate utility or 'pay-off' to agent i, given *all* of these actions, by $R_i(a, s, z)$. Assume that agent i seeks to maximize the expected, subjectively discounted sum of these pay-offs, or

$$E\left\{\sum_{t=0}^{\infty} \beta^t R_i(a_t, s_t, z_t)\right\}. \tag{1}$$

---

3 This argument is elaborated and illustrated with examples in Robert E. Lucas, Jr, 'Econometric policy evaluation: a critique', in *The Phillips Curve and Labor Markets*, Vol. 1 of the Carnegie–Rochester Series on Public Policy, Karl Brunner and Allan H. Meltzer (eds) (North-Holland, Amsterdam, 1976), pp. 19–46.

For (1) to be meaningful, the content of the operator $E\{\cdot\}$ must be specified. I will assume that expectations are *rational* in John Muth's sense, or that agents *know* the functions $a(\cdot)$ and $z(\cdot)$, and the distribution defined by F and G of the state vectors s_t, and that they take the expectation $E\{\cdot\}$ correctly.[4] For this discussion, I will assume that all agents have the common information s_t at each date t, so that $E\{\}$ means an expectation conditioned on the initial information s_0.

A central construct in discussing agent i's decision problem is his *value function* $v_i(s)$, interpreted as the value of his objective function (1) when the system begins in state s, and he chooses the optimal action a_i from the set Ω_i. This value function must satisfy a 'Bellman equation' (after the late mathematician Richard Bellman), which we can derive by thinking through the consequences of a particular a_i choice. The *immediate* payoff of such a choice, the first term in the sum (1), is just $R_i(a, s, z(s))$. The longer-term consequences, the remaining terms in (1), are

4 John F. Muth, 'Rational expectations and the theory of price movements', *Econometrica* **29** (1961), pp. 315–35. The term 'rational expectations', as Muth used it, refers to a consistency axiom for economic models, so it can be given precise meaning only in the context of specific models. I think this is why attempts to define rational expectations in a model-free way tend to come out either vacuous ('People do the best they can with the information they have') or silly ('People know the true structure of the world they live in').

[13]

summarized by $\beta E\{v_i(s')\}$: the value of the agent's objective as of the beginning of *next* period, when the state is s' (an expectation, since s' is not perfectly predictable), discounted to the present by the discount factor β. Now s' is determined in part by the agent's own action a_i, in part by other agents' actions, a_{-i}, and in part by nature: $s' = H(z(s), a, s, e)$. Optimal behavior means maximizing the sum of immediate and long-term pay-offs, and it yields the value $v_i(s)$. The Bellman equation is thus:

$$v_i(s) = \max_{a_i \in \Omega_i(a_{-i}, s, z)} \{R_i(a, s, z)$$

$$+ \beta \int v_i(H(z(s), a, s, e)) dG(e)\}. \qquad (2)$$

The system (2) for $i = 1, \ldots, n$ is in *equilibrium* when each agent i chooses the action a_i that attains the right side of (2), given the actions $(a_1, \ldots, a_{i-1}, a_{i+1}, \ldots, a_n) = a_{-i}$ chosen by all other agents. Clearly the nature of such an equilibrium $a(s) = (a_1(s), \ldots, a_n(s))$ will depend on everything that determines the nature of this game: the return functions R_i, the opportunity sets Ω_i, the function generating policies, $z(s)$, and the law of motion H, G of the system as a whole. Any *change* in policy, in the sense of a change in the function $z(\cdot)$ that describes the way policy variables react to the state of the system, will induce changes in the solution functions $a(\cdot)$, and hence in the reduced form behavior $F(\cdot)$ of the system as a whole.

[14]

For a model of the form (2) to be useful in evaluating policies, it is essential in the first place that we be able to calculate the solution functions $v_1, ..., v_n$. There is certainly no generally useful algorithm for doing this, and as we shall see, successful applications to date involve imposing stringent restrictions on the formulation to give tractability. This is a mathematical frontier on which there is much to be done. Even if (2) can be solved, the system will be successful in simulating policy effects only if the preferences R_i and the technology and rules of the game Ω_i are invariant under changes in policy z. This property is not one that can be guaranteed logically: if it could, we would not need to *test* economic models but could simply build them up from impeccable axioms. Of course, in practice all axioms for models we can actually solve will be crude approximations at best, and determining which axioms produce reliable models will involve judgement, testing and luck.

I have deliberately set out this formalism without saying anything at all specific about the nature of the 'game' agents are assumed to 'play' at each date t. I have described the actions a_i simultaneously chosen by agents as a (Nash) *equilibrium*, but the term equilibrium in this (now entirely standard) context obviously does not refer to a system 'at rest', nor does it necessarily mean 'competitive' equilibrium in the sense of price taking agents, nor does it have in general any connection with social optimality properties of any

[15]

kind. All it *does* mean is that, in the model, the objectives of each agent and the situation he faces are made explicit, that each agent is doing the best he can in light of the actions taken by others, and that these actions taken together are technologically feasible.

It is not going to be possible to say anything very specific about business cycles or about stabilization policy at this level of generality, so I will soon consider much more specific (and controversial) models. But the main criticisms of Keynesian models and their use in formulating policies that one associates with the idea of 'rational expectations' are all straightforward consequences of the acceptance of the general formalism of dynamic games that I am using here. Let me review what these are.

Keynesian models – at least as this term was used in the 1960s and 1970s – consist of a set of equations most of which are the decision rules of agents, the functions $a_i(s)$ in my notation. That is, their structural equations describe the levels of consumption, investment, money demand, and so on, that agents choose as functions of variables describing their situation. Some equations also describe the decision rules of fictional agents, like the auctioneer who is assumed to move prices or wages in the 'Phillips curve'. This is the nature of the large-scale econometric models based on Keynesian ideas. It also describes textbook models of the 'IS-LM' variety, and their many theoretical refinements. Now over a period of time in which policies are generated (or can be viewed as generated) by a fixed function $z(s)$ one would expect the 'structure' $a(s)$ of such models to remain fixed as well, and hence also $F(s, e) = H(z(s), a(s), s, e)$. Then forecasts based on this reduced form F should be accurate (up to unavoidable errors due to unpredictable e_t shocks). On the other hand, an attempt to simulate the effects of policy *changes* – changes in the *function* $z(s)$ – carried out by holding $a(s)$ fixed, will not yield accurate answers as long as equation (2) holds. I think the general logic of this criticism is widely understood. Its practical significance was dramatically illustrated by the failure of models containing 'stable' Phillips curves to deal with the effects of 1970s inflation, but the point is obviously not specific to this particular relationship.

If one had an accurate model of the form (2), simulations of a change in $z(s)$ to $z'(s)$ could be carried out accurately by substituting $z'(s)$ for $z(s)$ in (2), re-solving the system for new equilibrium decision rules $a'(s)$, and using this new *pair* (z', a') to describe the new motion $s_{t+1} = H(z'(s_t), a'(s_t), s_t, e_t)$ of the system. That is, one would assess policies by working out the equilibrium of the new 'game' they imply. I do not see any way short of this to estimate the likely effects of policy changes.

These remarks refer to correct and incorrect ways of simulating the effects of changes in some *function* $z(s)$ that is assumed to generate individual

[17]

policy decisions z_t, so the thought-experiment involves a once-and-for-all change from one fixed function z to another, z'. Examples of such a policy shift would be a shift from a monetary policy directed at stabilizing interest rates to one directed at achieving a money growth target, or from a fiscal policy directed at budget balancing to one directed at some kind of 'leaning against the wind'. Yet in general, at least since the Second World War, macroeconomic policy is not discussed in terms of functions or rules at all, but in terms of selecting current policy *numbers:* this year's deficit, this year's money growth, and so on. The idea – formalized in the USA in the Employment Act of 1946 – is that policy ought not to be pre-set in *any* sense, but rather that government should have broad discretion to deal with each year's unique economic situation as it arises.

The framework I have just described does not equip the economic expert to participate in this kind of policy discussion. According to (2), agents will *have* to form an opinion as to how *future* policy is to be made in order to decide how to react to *current* policies. If an expert is asked to predict how people will react to a particular choice of z_t independent of the way future z_t-values are to be chosen, he will simply have to say that he doesn't know, or else reformulate the question to the point where it has an answer.

This is what I meant in my introduction when I said that modern theoretical developments lead to radical changes in the way we think about policy. If the viewpoint of dynamic games, in any form, is a useful way of thinking about policy then the use of Keynesian models to set policy on a year-to-year basis is not. Trying to reconcile these two points of view by interpreting ideas based on rational expectations as an alternative way of solving the year-to-year management problems to which the Keynesian framework addresses itself will just lead to confusion and misunderstanding. I will come back to this at the conclusion of the lectures, when I will summarize what I think economic theory *does* have to say about economic policy.

III

If we are to move beyond the general formalism I have been discussing to models that account for specific features of business cycles, it will be necessary to be more specific about the agents in the system, about the technology at their disposal, and about the way they interact. In this section, I will consider consumer preferences only, saying nothing about the other, much more difficult, aspects of the problem. It is remarkable how much one can say about the importance of macroeconomic questions on the basis of preferences alone.

Any economic model is going to have at its center a collection of hypothetical consumers whose decisions, together with the technology and market structure, determine the operating characteristics of the system and whose welfare is the explicit subject of normative analysis. A typical household will consume a collection c_t of goods at date t, possibly contingent on probabilistically-determined events between dates zero and t, and will evaluate an entire sequence, or process, $\{c_t\}$ of consumption according to a utility function such as (1), specialized here to:

$$E\left\{\sum_{t=0}^{\infty}\beta^t U(c_t)\right\} \tag{3}$$

If we are to think about economic policy starting from this viewpoint, what we mean, in the first place, is that we want the ability to be able to determine how different policies will induce different consumption sequences $\{c_{it}\}$ for each agent i in this economy. In the second place, we mean to evaluate policies normatively according to their effects on agents' welfare as measured by (3).

We can move to some sharper, quantitative conclusions for macroeconomic problems if we abstract from issues involving the *mix* of consumption goods at date t and limit discussion to policies affecting consumption of goods-in-general. At the simplest level, let us identify c_t with real consumption at date t, and specialize preferences to:

$$E\left\{\sum_{t=0}^{\infty}\beta^t \frac{1}{1-\sigma}(c_t^{1-\sigma}-1)\right\} \tag{4}$$

where $\beta\in(0, 1)$ is a constant discount factor and $\sigma>0$ is the constant coefficient of relative risk-aversion. This two-parameter preference family will not be adequate for every problem I will want to address, but it will serve to get the discussion going in a concrete way.

[21]

Before situating this consumer (4) in a model of the sort outlined in Section II, let us examine his attitudes toward some purely hypothetical consumption streams by simply *asking* him about them. Since I am particularly interested in his attitudes toward growth and fluctuations, it will be useful to work with a class of consumption streams with 'trend' and 'cycle' components, such as:

$$c_t = (1 + \lambda)(1 + \mu)^t e^{-\frac{1}{2}\sigma_z^2} z_t, \; t = 0, 1, \ldots, \tag{5}$$

where $\{z_t\}$ is a stationary stochastic process with a stationary distribution given by:

$$\ln(z_t) \sim N(O, \sigma_z^2).$$

Then $E(e^{-\frac{1}{2}\sigma_z^2} z_t) = 1$, so that mean consumption under these assumptions is $(1 + \lambda)(1 + \mu)^t$.[1] Setting

1 The assumption that mean consumption follows a deterministic trend, and hence is perfectly predictable, is not innocuous in this context, and it would be desirable to work through the calculations below under alternative assumptions. Charles R. Nelson and Charles I. Plosser, 'Trends and random walks in macroeconomic time series, some evidence and implications', *Journal of Monetary Economics* **10** (1981), pp. 139–62, have recently argued that most year-to-year variability in US real GNP can be attributed to a random walk, or stochastic trend, component. It is likely that similar methods applied to consumption would lead to a similar conclusion. I agree with John H. Cochrane, 'How big is the random walk in GNP?' (University of Chicago Work ing Paper, 1986) that Nelson and Plosser's methods have considerably overstated the importance of the random walk component, but even so it seems clear that something inter-

[22]

the parameter λ is just a matter of units: I will use it later on to provide 'compensation' for variations in the parameters μ and σ_z^2. For the USA the annual growth rate in total consumption is about 3 per cent, so $\mu = 0.03$ can serve as a benchmark value. For the post-war period in the USA the standard deviation of the log of consumption about trend is about 0.013 (so that average consumption that is as much as 2.5 per cent above or below trend is a 'two-sigma' event), so that $\sigma_z^2 = (0.013)^2$ is a benchmark value.[2] Thus we may take (5) with $(\lambda, \mu, \sigma_z^2) = (0, 0.03, (0.013)^2)$ as a rough description of the consumption behavior the average American family is used to, and examine its attitudes toward changes.

Given any choice of $(\lambda, \mu, \sigma_z^2)$ we could simply calculate the value of (4) under the consumption

mediate to Nelson and Plosser's model and (5) would provide a better description of consumption behavior than (5) does.

2 This figure is from Finn E. Kydland and Edward C. Prescott, 'Time to build and aggregate fluctuations', *Econometrica* **50** (1982), pp. 1345-70, table IV, p. 1365. Since 0.013 is a quarterly figure, it overstates the standard deviation of annual consumption, but not by much, since consumption is highly serially correlated. This number and others used in this section are intended to give a rough idea of the relative importance of certain issues. The reader will agree, I think, upon reaching the end of the section that its conclusions do not hinge on delicate questions of measurement.

behavior (5) and call the indirect utility function so defined $U(\lambda, \mu, \sigma_z^2)$. But we will obtain a measure that is easier to think about if we use *compensating variations* in λ to evaluate various μ and σ_z^2 changes. To evaluate changes in the growth rate μ, for example, let us define $f(\mu, \mu_0)$ by:

$$U(f(\mu, \mu_0), \mu, \sigma_z^2) = U(0, \mu_0, \sigma_z^2), \tag{6}$$

so that $f(\mu, \mu_0)$ is the percentage change in consumption, uniform across all dates and values of the shocks, required to leave the consumer indifferent between the growth rates μ and μ_0. (In general, σ_z^2 would appear as an argument of f, too, but under these 'constant relative risk-aversion' preferences it drops out.) A direct calculation gives:

$$f(\mu, \mu_0) = \left(\frac{1 + \mu_0}{1 + \mu}\right)^{\beta/(1 - \beta)} - 1.$$

Here is a table of this function f, which I will call simply the *cost* of reduced growth, for $\beta = 0.95$ and a base growth rate of $\mu_0 = 0.03$.

At the parameters used in table 1, then, consumers would require a 20 per cent across-the-board consumption increase to accept voluntarily a reduction in the consumption growth rate from 0.03 to 0.02, and would surrender 42 per cent across the board to obtain an increase in the growth rate from 0.03 to 0.06.

I hasten to add that I have said nothing about the *feasibility* of these growth rate changes; I am

[24]

TABLE 1   Cost of reducing growth from $\mu_0 = 0.03$ when $\beta = 0.95$

μ	$f(\mu, \mu_0)$
0.01	0.45
0.02	0.20
0.03	0.00
0.04	− 0.17
0.05	− 0.31
0.06	− 0.42

simply running experiments on this fictional consumer. Indeed, under a standard, neoclassical technology, policies that affect growth usually do so only over a transient period only, not permanently as in table 1. But the range of growth rates in table 1 is not large relative to what we observe across countries, and the welfare consequences of 'small' changes are *enormous*, relative to anything we will see in what follows. I shall return to this later on.

The costs of economic instability can be measured in a way that is identical conceptually to this way of measuring the costs of reduced growth. To this end, define the function $g(\sigma_z^2)$ by

$$U(g(\sigma_z^2), \mu, \sigma_z^2) = U(0, \mu, 0). \tag{7}$$

That is, $g(\sigma_z^2)$ is the percentage increase in consumption, uniform across all dates and values of

[25]

the shocks, required to leave the consumer indifferent between consumption instability of σ_z^2 and a *perfectly* smooth consumption path. I will call $g(\sigma_z^2)$ the cost of consumption instability.

By direct calculation, and using the approximation $\ln(1 + \lambda) = \lambda$ (which is entirely safe in this context), g is given by:

$$g(\sigma_z^2) \cong \tfrac{1}{2}\sigma \cdot \sigma_z^2. \tag{8}$$

Table 2 shows the function g, for various σ and σ_z^2 values. The coefficient σ of risk-aversion can be estimated from a variety of different samples: estimates vary widely. A value of unity means logarithmic preferences; people appear to be more risk-averse than this. No available estimates are as large as 20, but some do exceed 10.

The value 0.013 is the standard deviation of the log of US real quarterly consumption, expressed as a deviation from fitted trend, over the period following the Second World War. Eliminating

TABLE 2   Cost of consumption instability: $g(\sigma_z^2)$

σ	σ_z		
	0.013	*0.039*	*0.120*
1	0.00008	0.00072	0.0065
5	0.00042	0.0038	0.034
10	0.00084	0.0076	0.068
20	0.0017	0.015	0.136

aggregate consumption variability of this magnitude entirely, would, from table 2, be the equivalent in utility terms of an increase in *average* consumption of something less than one tenth of a percentage point. (Total US consumption in 1983 was $2 trillion, so one-tenth of 1 per cent is $2 billion, which sounds like a sizeable free lunch. But there were 234 million people to feed, so lunch will have to run about $8.50 per person.) I want to propose taking these numbers seriously as giving the order-of-magnitude of the potential marginal social product of additional advances in business cycle theory – or more accurately, as a loose upper bound, since there is no reason to think that eliminating *all* consumption variability is either a feasible or a desirable objective of policy. But I imagine that even one-tenth of a percentage point will seem to many to be an extremely low estimate of the costs of economic instability – at least, it did to me – so it will be useful to digress to discuss some aspects of this estimate.[3]

---

3 The estimates in table 2 appear somewhat less surprisingly low when compared to estimates of the welfare gains from other (also purely hypothetical) policy changes. For example, Arnold C. Harberger, 'Monopoly and resource allocation', *American Economic Review* **44** (1954), pp. 77–87, found one-tenth of 1 per cent of income to be an upper bound on the welfare gain from the (costless) elimination of *all* product market monopoly in the US economy. Harberger, too, was led to 'confess that I was amazed at this result' (p. 86), but it has not been revised upward by any

The last two columns of table 2 set up what seem to me the two most important qualifications or elaborations of this cost estimate. First, in the period prior to the Second World War, and extending as far back in time as we have usable data, the standard deviation (logarithmic deviations from trend) of consumption was about three times its post-war level.[4] Since this number is squared in the

---

quantitative research I have seen in the 30 years since his study was published. Perhaps we should be open to the possibility that the intrinsic importance of substantive economic questions is not accurately reflected by the number of journal pages devoted to them.

It is not quite accurate to identify instability in goods consumption with economic instability in general, since consumption of leisure also fluctuates. But since hours worked and goods consumption are positively correlated cyclically, I would guess that taking leisure fluctuations into account more carefully would *reduce* the estimates in the text still further.

4 In a recent paper, Christina Romer, 'Spurious volatility in historical unemployment data', *Journal of Political Economy* **94** (1986, 1–37), has argued that pre-First (not second) World War variability in unemployment rates was, correctly measured, no larger than post-Second World War variability. It appears from related work of hers that the amplitudes of other series (probably including real consumption) were also badly overstated in pre-First World War data. The statement in the text may then rest much more heavily on the experience of the 1930s than I would previously have thought. It would be hard to overstate the importance of the questions on which these findings bear, but I have not attempted to incorporate them into my illustrative calculations.

[28]

formula (8), the implied cost estimates are multiplied by nine, becoming something like one-half of 1 per cent of total consumption. As deadweight losses go, *this* is a large number. Second, fluctuations in total consumption do not affect all households equiproportionally, so that variability of total consumption does not capture anything like all of the consumption risk faced by the typical household. Perhaps correcting for this effect would lead to another tripling of the relevant standard deviation, and hence another multiplication by nine in the cost estimates. This is the last column of table 2.

But as a measure of the possible gains from improvements in aggregative policy, this last column is way too high. In so far as the absence of income-risk pooling reflects 'imperfections' in capital markets, and I think it does, the cost of *individual* income variability measures the potential or actual gain from social insurance, not from stabilization policy. Aggregate income variability is but one source of individual income risk, and reduction of aggregate variability – which is all that stabilization policies can accomplish – cannot be expected to eliminate more than a small part of the uninsurable risk borne at the individual level. I will return to the issue of social insurance later on, in section V, when we have invested in a framework more suitable for posing questions about individual earnings risk and ways of dealing with it.

An economic system is a collection of people and serious evaluation of economic policy involves tracing the consequences of policies back to the welfare of the individuals they affect. Without saying much more about the nature or workings of the economy than this, we can get a good if rough idea of the potential benefit of policies that alter individual consumption streams in various ways. I have run through two exercises to assess the potential welfare gains of policies that affect the growth of consumption and policies that affect the variability of consumption about its trend, not by describing policies that would have these effects, but simply by imagining that these effects somehow come about. It is worth re-emphasizing that these calculations rest on assumptions about preferences *only*, and not about any particular mechanism – equilibrium or disequilibrium – assumed to generate business cycles.

I find the exercise instructive, for it indicates that economic instability at the level we have experienced since the Second World War is a minor problem, even relative to historically experienced inflation[5] and certainly relative to the costs

5 In Robert E. Lucas, Jr, 'Discussion of: Stanley Fischer, "Towards an understanding of the costs of inflation: II"', *Carnegie–Rochester Conference Series on Public Policy* **15** (1981), pp. 43–50, I estimated the annual social cost of a sustained 10 per cent inflation in the USA to be 0.5 per cent of national income. The estimate follows the method used in Martin J. Bailey, 'The welfare cost of inflationary finance', *Journal of Political Economy* **64** (1956), pp. 93–110, and uses the interest elasticity of money demand estimates in

of modestly reduced rates of economic growth. This is not to say that economic fluctuations are a trivial problem, for fluctuations at the pre-Second World War level, especially combined as they were with an absence of adequate programs for social insurance, were associated with large costs in welfare. But it suggests that the main social gains from a deeper understanding of business cycles, whatever form this deeper understanding may take, will be in helping us to see how to avoid large mistakes with policies that have minimally inefficient side-effects, not in devising ever more subtle policies to remove the residual amount of business-cycle risk.

Phillip Cagan, 'The monetary dynamics of hyperinflation', in Milton Friedman (ed.) *Studies in the Quantity Theory of Money* (University of Chicago Press, Chicago, 1956).

IV

It is possible to get a rough idea of the order of magnitude of the potential gains in welfare from stabilization policies by the method of the preceding discussion, and I thought this exercise would be a useful preliminary. But to go beyond the calculation of crude upper bounds it will be necessary to take a position on the way the economy actually works, or to construct a positive theory of business cycles. In this section, I will turn to the discussion of a simple prototype model that I think holds much promise for future developments.

There are many interesting prototype business cycles models in existence now, and I have no doubt that many of them will contribute, in different ways, to the development of improved future models. Of these, the most useful for the present discussion is one introduced recently by Kydland and Prescott.[1] This model focuses exclusively on

1 Kydland and Prescott, 'Time to build and aggregate fluctuations'. Technically, the immediate ancestor of Kydland and Prescott is William A. Brock and Leonard Mir-

real (as opposed to monetary) neoclassical considerations, which I think is a mistake, but it is the
only model I know of that is theoretically coherent
in the sense we discussed in section II, while yet
having been developed to the point where its
implications can be compared to observed time
series in a quantitatively serious way.[2]

The Kydland and Prescott model is a highly
simplified, competitive system, in which a single
good is produced by labor and capital with a constant returns technology. All consumers are
assumed to be infinitely-lived and identical. The
only 'shocks' to the system are exogenous, stochastic shifts in the production technology. Kydland

---

man, 'Optimal economic growth and uncertainty: the
discounted case', *Journal of Economic Theory* 4 (1972), pp.
479–513.

2 Two other interesting prototypes that have been
compared to actual time-series data are described in
Thomas J. Sargent, 'A classical macroeconometric model for
the United States', *Journal of Political Economy* 84 (1976),
pp. 207–38; and John B. Taylor, 'Estimation and control of a
macroeconomic model with rational expectations', *Econometrica* 47 (1979), pp. 1267–86. These models have the
advantage of incorporating monetary as well as real disturbances, but since neither explicitly relates its structure to
assumptions about technology and preferences, they are
more difficult to relate to the theoretical structure I sketched
in section II. On the other hand, illustrative models like that
in Robert E. Lucas, Jr, 'Expectations and the neutrality of
money', *Journal of Economic Theory* 4 (1972), pp. 103–24,
are too abstract to be compared in any detail to observed
aggregate time-series.

and Prescott ask the question: 'Can specific parametric descriptions of technology and preferences be found such that the movements induced in output, consumption, employment and other series in such a model by these exogenous shocks resemble the time series behavior of the observed counterparts to these series in the postwar, US economy?' This seems to me exactly the right question for macroeconomists to ask, and I want to discuss three aspects of Kydland and Prescott's answer to it: (1) the methods they used to carry out the simulation; (2) the way they make the critical term 'resemble' operational; and (3) the success the model can claim as an explanation for business cycles.

In describing the model, it will be easiest to begin with a system that is simpler than the one Kydland and Prescott used, and then to describe their model as a variation on this simpler one. Let the typical household be endowed with $\bar{n}$ units of time each period, and let its current period utility depend on goods c_t consumed and 'leisure' $\bar{n} - n_t$, where n_t is labor sold to firms. Preferences are assumed to be:

$$E\left\{\sum_{t=0}^{\infty} \beta^t U(c_t, \bar{n} - n_t)\right\}.$$

The technology is $F(k_t, n_t, x_t)$, where the value of F is the units of output that can be produced with k_t units of capital, and n_t man-hours of labor

[34]

when the stochastic technology shock is x_t. These shocks x_t follow a Markov process with transitions

$$G(x', x) = Pr\{x_{t+1} \leqslant x' \mid x_t = x\}.$$

F is homogenous of degree one in (k_t, n_t), so we can interpret all variables in per-household terms. Output is divided into consumption c_t and gross investment i_t and capital evolves according to

$$k_{t+1} = i_t + (1 - \delta)k_t.$$

Households own all factors of production, renting them to profit-maximizing firms each period at wages and capital rentals w_t and u_t (with the price of current output normalized at unity). These markets are, as I have said, competitive. Households' expectations about future factor prices are rational. Once the functions U, F and G are specified (as Kydland and Prescott do) this is all that needs to be said: working out the predictions of the model is just a matter of technique.

But technique is interesting to technicians (which is what we are, if we are to be of any use to anyone) so let me go into a little more detail, by casting the decision problem faced by a typical household into the formalism I developed earlier. From the household's point of view, the state of this system is described at each date by three numbers: its own holdings of capital, y (say), the capital stock in the economy as a whole, k, and the current technology shock, x. (In equilibrium, we know that y and k will have to be equal – otherwise the typical household would not be typical – but this equality cannot be *imposed* on the household: prices have to move to make equality *desirable* to it.) Then the state s of the system will be this triple (y, k, x). I will work toward a statement of the Bellman equation for the household's value function $v(s)$.

At each date, the action a chosen by the household (since all households are alike, we don't need the subscript i) is the triple (c, n, y') describing its consumption, labor supply and end-of-period capital holdings. The immediate return from any such action is just $R(a) = U(c, \bar{n} - n)$. The opportunity set Ω from which an action is selected is determined by the current factor prices $w(k, x)$, $u(k, x)$ (or $w(s)$, $u(s)$) which depend on the economy's state (k, x), but *not* on the individual's holdings y: this is what competition means, in this context. Thus:

$$\Omega(y, k, x) = \{(c, n, y'): c + y' \leqslant w(k, x)n + u(k, x)y$$

$$+ (1 - \delta)y, c \geqslant 0,$$

$$0 \leqslant n \leqslant \bar{n}, y' \geqslant (1 - \delta)y\}.$$

In an equilibrium, the next period capital stock for the economy as a whole, k', will be some function $h(k, x)$ of today's state. Rational expectations implies that this function is known by agents, along with the functions G, w and u. Then $v(s)$ must satisfy:

[36]

$$v(s) = \max_{(c,\,n,\,y')\in\Omega} \{U(c, \bar{n} - n)$$

$$+ \beta \int v(y', h(k, x), x')dG(x', x)\}, \qquad (9)$$

where Ω is the set defined above. Equation (9) thus describes the decision problem faced by a household deciding on its consumption, labor supply and savings, given current factor prices $w(s)$ and $u(s)$ and given expectations about the way these prices will behave in the future. These expectations, in turn, can be calculated from knowledge about the current state of the system, (k, x), the way the distribution G of future exogenous shocks depends on this state, and the way the capital stock of the economy evolves, h.

If households behave according to (9), their decisions (c, n, y') will be fixed functions of the state (y, k, x) that sets the terms of this maximum problem. In particular, the household's own capital holdings will evolve according to a difference equation:

$$y_{t+1} = y(y_t, k_t, x_t),$$

where the function $y(\cdot)$ can be obtained from the study of the maximum problem (9). The economy's capital stock, we have assumed, evolves according to:

$$k_{t+1} = h(k_t, x_t).$$

In equilibrium, it must be the case that $k_t = y_t$ for all t (that is, that all capital is held) which thus

[37]

translates into the condition that $y(k, k, x) = h(k, x)$, identically in (k, x). That is to say, the system is in a rational expectations equilibrium when the savings behavior each household *believes* others will follow coincides with the savings behavior each household finds it optimal to follow, given its expectations about others.

In fact, Kydland and Prescott did not proceed directly to solve (9) and to construct the equilibrium function h in the way I have just sketched. Instead, they calculated solutions to the planning problem:

$$f(k, x) = \max_{c, n, k'} \{U(c, \bar{n} - n) + \beta \int f(k', x') G(dx', x)\}$$

(10)

subject to $c \geq 0$, $0 \leq n \leq \bar{n}$, $k' \geq (1 - \delta)k$, and

$$k' + c' \leq F(k, n, x) + (1 - \delta)k.$$

Equation (10) describes the behavior of a planner deciding on households' consumption, labor supply and capital accumulation, given constraints imposed by the technology F and the current shock x. It is a classical fact that the optimal capital accumulation behavior $k_{t+1} = h(k_t, x_t)$ for this hypothetical planning problem *coincides* with the competitive equilibrium accumulation behavior I have just described.[3] The study of (10) thus

3 Gerard Debreu, 'Valuation equilibrium and Pareto optimum', *Proceedings of the National Academy of Sciences* **40** (1954), pp. 588–92.

provides an indirect method for calculating the function h describing the competitive equilibrium motion of the endogenous state variables in an inexpensive way, sidestepping the simultaneity I discussed above.

Having obtained numerical solutions to the model in this way, the equilibrium behavior of the capital stock can be simulated by drawing shocks $\{x_t\}$ from the assumed distribution $G(x', x)$ and running the difference equation $k_{t+1} = h(k_t, x_t)$. Since the values of consumption, employment and factor prices are all given by the theory as functions of (k_t, x_t), the model generates time series for these variables as well. This is precisely the method Slutsky used in his 1927 paper,[4] in which he demonstrated for the first time that stochastic difference equation systems could generate behavior that closely resembled economic time series. The difference is that in this case the function $h(\cdot)$ has a clear economic interpretation in terms of preferences and technology.

The artificial time series so generated by the theoretical model 'look like' economic time series in the sense that the series Slutsky generated did: the variables show erratic, serially correlated fluctuations about their mean values. This much could be guessed from the economics of the model's

4 Eugenio Slutsky, 'The summation of random causes as the source of cyclic processes', *Econometrica* **5** (1937), pp. 105–46.

structure: a favorable technology shock shifts out current production possibilities; this induces high capital accumulation which spreads this benefit forward into future periods. But a more detailed comparison of the artificially generated series with their observed counterparts is not so encouraging. The employment movements predicted by the model have lower amplitude (relative to output movements) than do actual employment variations. Consumption is more volatile and investment much less so in the model as compared to actual data.

To deal with these discrepancies, Kydland and Prescott's published model used a modified formulation of both preferences and technology. For preferences, the 'leisure' argument $\bar{n} - n_t$ in current utility was replaced with a distributed lag of current *and* past values of $\bar{n} - n_t$. This has the effect of increasing the degree of *intertemporal substitutability* of leisure without altering the assumed intertemporal substitutability of consumption.[5] On the technology side, the assumption

5 Gary D. Hansen, 'Indivisible labor and the business cycle', *Journal of Monetary Economics* **16** (1985), pp. 309–28; and William Rogerson, 'Indivisible labor, lotteries, and the business cycle', unpublished University of Rochester work ing paper (1985), have modified the preference structure described above in a different direction, by assuming that household must supply labor in an all-or-nothing fashion, so that a 10 per cent decrease in aggregate labor supply comes about by a 100 per cent reduction in the labor supplied by

that investment at date t augments the stock of productive capital at date $t + 1$ was replaced with a gestation lag scheme with the property that an investment project initiated at date t comes to completion at date $t + \tau$, τ fixed, with investment expenditures being incurred at all dates in between. The nature of the technology shock was also altered somewhat, so that it is assumed to consist of 'permanent' (that is, highly persistent) and transient components, in a mix that cannot be observed by agents. The effect of these modifications is to increase the dimension of the state space in which s_t lies, and markedly to improve the model's ability to fit data. The underlying logic of the model and its solution method remains, however, exactly as I have described.

It is instructive to run a simulated 'boom' through the Kydland and Prescott model. Suppose a high technology shock occurs, increasing the current productivity of both capital and labor. This makes the current period attractive to work and produce, relative to conditions that are expected to prevail in future periods, so both employment and output rise. It also *may* signal high productivity in

10 per cent of households, rather than a 10 per cent reduction by all households. It is remarkable (but true) that this variation, in some ways more realistic, can still be analyzed within an identical-household framework. Hansen's work shows that a Kydland–Prescott model, so modified, permits much higher employment variability than even the modified Kydland–Prescott model as reported in tables 3 and 4.

[41]

future periods, and the only way for firms to hedge against this (attractive) contingency is to initiate investment projects now. The projects so initiated will operate to increase output and employment until they are completed, spreading the effects of this shock – even if it should turn out after the fact to be transient – forward into future periods. They also carry within them the seeds of a future downturn, both because they increase the capital stock – possibly inappropriately – and because workers will be less willing to supply labor in future periods, having extended themselves in sustaining the boom.

Can such a scenario generate the investment-dominated fluctuations we seem to observe? It is hard to tell: the interactions are too complicated, even in so stripped-down a model, to work out in one's head or with pencil and paper. To pursue this question more systematically, Kydland and Prescott began by estimating as many parameters as possible from a wide variety of out-of-sample evidence. For example, the fact that people work about one-third of the time pinned down one preference parameter; the observation that investment projects take something like a year to complete was used to fix a technological parameter; and so forth. Having estimated as many parameters as they could in this way, without even looking at the time series they were attempting to fit, the number of free parameters – including the critical parameters characterizing the technology shocks

[42]

that drive the system – was reduced to about six. Kydland and Prescott then chose values for these remaining parameters so as to make certain low order moments (variances, covariances, autovariances) predicted by the model 'match' the corresponding moments from the collection of time series in the sample they used. The result of this last step completed the estimation, and the matches between the theoretical and actual moments they reported are the only reported 'test' of the model's ability to 'fit' these series.

Tables 3 and 4 summarize some of the main features of the comparisons reported by Kydland and Prescott. Both tables compare sample moments to moments implied by the estimated model for deviations of the indicated series about a fitted trend. In the simulations underlying these tables, the variance of the technology shocks was chosen so as to make the standard deviations

TABLE 3   Auto-correlations of output

Time lag (quarters)	Model	US economy 1950–79
1	0.71	0.84
2	0.45	0.57
3	0.28	0.27
4	0.19	− 0.01
5	0.02	− 0.20
6	− 0.13	− 0.30

[43]

TABLE 4 Standard deviations and correlations with real output

Variable	Model		US economy	
	Standard deviation	Correlation with output	Standard deviation	Correlation with output
Real GNP	1.8	–	1.8	–
Consumption (non-durable)	0.9	0.66	0.6	0.94
Investment	6.4	0.80	5.1	0.71
Man-hours	1.0	0.93	2.0	0.85

(about trend) for real GNP for the model equal to its value for the post-war US economy: this is not a test of the model. The difficult moments to fit (simultaneously) are the standard deviations of consumption, investment and man-hours, and the formulations of preferences and technology that I described a moment ago are motivated exactly to bring these three predictions into closer correspondence to what we observe.

Whether these results are viewed as 'good' or 'bad' is a difficult question, as is the related question of which comparisons of theoretical to sample moments are most interesting. One could obtain a formal sharpening of these questions by using the discipline of classical hypothesis testing (and a recent paper by Sumru Altug shows that this route is indeed instructive[6]) but the interesting question raised by the Kydland and Prescott model is surely not whether it can be accepted as 'true' when nested within some broader class of models. Of course the model is not 'true': this much is evident from the axioms on which it is constructed. We know from the outset in an enterprise like this (I would say, in *any* effort in positive economics) that what will emerge – *at best* – is a workable approximation that is useful in answering a limited set of questions.

6 Sumru Altug, 'Estimation and Tests of an Aggregate Equilibrium Model', unpublished Federal Reserve Bank of Minneapolis working paper, 1985.

[45]

Kydland and Prescott do not say much about which questions they hope their model could simulate accurately, or with what level of accuracy, but the model is set up to focus on the way firms and consumers react to changes in the intertemporal pattern of actual and expected prices: hence their focus on the opportunities agents have for substituting across time – for working now and postponing leisure, for initiating investment now as opposed to waiting for more information, and so on. They parameterize as many of these trade-offs as they can in such a way as to facilitate bringing as wide a variety of evidence as possible to bear on these questions. Thus the coefficient of risk-aversion in consumer preferences can be deduced from cross-section patterns in risk premia as well as from investments in aggregate consumption, the gestation lags for investment projects can be observed directly, at least for some kinds of investment, and so on. This is the point of 'microeconomic foundations' of macroeconomic models: to discover parameterizations that have interpretations in terms of specific aspects of preferences or of technology, so that the broadest range of evidence can be brought to bear on their magnitudes and their stability under various possible conditions.

Kydland and Prescott have taken macroeconomic modeling into new territory, with a formulation that combines intelligible general equilibrium theory with an operational, empirical seriousness

[46]

that rivals at least early versions of Keynesian macroeconometric models. Exactly *because* their model carries predictions for so wide a range of evidence, it has been subjected to an unusually wide range of empirically-based criticism: here is a macroeconomic model that actually makes contact with microeconomic studies in labor economics! The chances that the model will survive this criticism unscathed are negligible, but this seems to me exactly what explicit theory is for, that is, to lay bare the assumptions about behavior on which the model rests, to bring evidence to bear on these assumptions, to revise them when needed, and so on.

The Kydland and Prescott model is another in a long and honorable (though recently dormant) line of real business-cycle models. Substantively, the model reopens a debate that played an important role in pre-Keynesian theory – a debate that Haberler surveyed so masterfully in *Prosperity and Depression*.[7] But this time around, the terms of the discussion are explicit and quantitative, and the relationship between theory and evidence can be (and is being) argued at an entirely different level. I would like to call this progress.

7 Gottfried Haberler, *Prosperity and Depression* (League of Nations, Geneva, 1937).

[47]

V

Kydland and Prescott frame the problem of explaining business cycles as one of accounting for volatility in employment and real output, and this is the viewpoint that I prefer too. This way of setting the question has led to the formulation of competitive models that exhibit such volatility, models in which quantities and prices are 'market clearing' in the sense of Walras. In most such models unemployment as a distinct activity plays no role whatever.

For many other economists, explaining business cycles is taken to *mean* accounting for recurrent episodes of widespread unemployment. From this alternative viewpoint, a model with cleared markets seems necessarily to miss the main point, however successful it may be at accounting for other phenomena, and the work of 'equilibrium' macroeconomists is often criticized as though it were a failed attempt to explain unemployment (which it surely does fail to do), instead of as an attempt to explain something else.[1]

As a matter of social science, the issue of whether to focus theoretically on unemployment or to focus on other features of business cycles and hope to learn something about unemployment as a by-product is one of research strategy, neither point of view being usefully enough developed at this point to have proved the other inferior. One of the purposes of this section will be to explain my viewpoint as part of a strategy to understand business cycles. But even if I am right in this strategy, there are clearly other questions, the determination of the best provision of unemployment insurance for example, for which unemployment is inescapably the central issue and from which one cannot abstract if any progress is to be made at all. For some purposes, then, a theory of unemployment is essential. In this section, I will sketch (entirely by borrowing from the existing literature) the main elements I think a useful theory must contain. Having done so, I will then turn to the question of whether incorporating such a theory into business cycle models at a macroeconomic level promises important new insights into the nature of business cycles.

Think, to begin with, about the Walrasian market for a vector of commodities, including as one component 'hours of labor services', that must

1 See, among many, many examples, James Tobin, *Asset Accumulation and Economic Activity*, Yrjö Jahnsson Lectures, 1978 (University of Chicago Press, Chicago, 1980), pp. 42ff.

[49]

be at the center of a competitive equilibrium model. In this scenario, households and firms submit supply and demand orders for labor services and other goods at various auctioneer-determined price vectors and, when a market-clearing price vector is found, trading is consummated at those prices. Each seller of labor sells as much or as little as he pleases at these prices, each is indifferent to the identity of the buyer(s) of the labor services he sells, and if this spot market is repeated at later dates, there is no reason to expect any continuity in the relationship between particular buyers and particular sellers. There is no sense in which anyone in this scenario can be said to 'have a job' or to lose, seek or find a job.

It seems clear enough that a model in which wages and hours of employment are set in this way can, *at best*, shed light on the determination of these two variables. Whatever success it may enjoy on these dimensions, it can tell us nothing about the list of labor market phenomena that have to do with sustained employer–employee relationships: their formation, their nature, their dissolution. In so far as these relationships are central to an understanding of business cycles, such a model will be inadequate to account for them. In any case, such a model clearly will not provide a useful account of observations on quits, fires, lay-offs and other phenomena that explicitly refer to aspects of the employer–employee relationship.

[50]

It is common, particularly in macroeconomic discussions, to summarize these inadequacies of models based on the Walrasian scenario by saying that they 'assume cleared markets' and, of course, they do. But this way of stating the problem has had the unfortunate consequence of suggesting to many that better models, models without these inadequacies, can be obtained simply by dropping the assumption of market clearing while retaining all other aspects of the Walras auction scenario.[2] In these 'fix-price' models, agents continue to submit sell orders for their labor services to the impersonal market, just as they do in an equilibrium model. Terms like employer, employee, quits and fires continue to have no counterpart in the theory. The *only* difference is that the auction terminates, and trading occurs, at some price vector *other* than the one that clears the market. The theory, so modified, loses whatever ability it had to account

2 See, for example, Robert Barro and Herschel Grossman, *Money, Employment, and Inflation* (Cambridge: Cambridge University Press, 1976); J. P. Benassy, 'Neo-Keynesian disequilibrium theory in a monetary economy', *Review of Economic Studies* (October 1975); J. Dreze, 'Existence of an exchange equilibrium under price rigidities', *International Economic Review* (June 1975); and Edmond Malinvaud, *The Theory of Unemployment Reconsidered*, Yrjö Jahnsson Lectures (Basil Blackwell, Oxford, 1977). I found Allan Drazen, 'Recent developments in macroeconomic disequilibrium theory', *Econometrica* **48** (March 1980), pp. 283–306, a useful recent survey of this literature.

for wage and employment determination in terms of preferences and technology. What does it gain in return?

The solution to the model now has a feature that can be described, without undue strain, as 'involuntary unemployment'. So the economic theory of the 1980s establishes at least verbal contact with the theory of the 1930s, but where is the contact between either theory and observed labor market behavior?[3] The difference between hours of labor services supplied at these non-market clearing prices and hours demanded is, if non-negative, identified as 'involuntary unemployment'. But why should this theoretical variable be identified with the observed survey-collected numbers we call 'unemployment?' There are no unemployed *people* in this Walrasian scenario, only unemployed hours of labor services. No one finds a job, or seeks one, or gets laid off from one. If one tries to imagine trying to *use* this model to design an unemployment compensation scheme, its sterility becomes evident. Benefits might as well be assigned to a seller of 40 hours per week, on the ground that he wished to sell 60, as to a seller of 10 hours. The fix-price model cannot help us get past

3 The first sentence in Malinvaud, *The Theory of Unemployment Reconsidered*, is: 'The term *involuntary* unemployment makes it obvious from the start that the labor market is one in which supply exceeds demand.' Thus we acquire factual information about labor markets from the terminology earlier theorists have used to describe them!

[52]

the limits of the Walrasian scenario on which the equilibrium models rest because it, too, accepts the Walrasian abstraction from any kind of continuing relationship between buyers and sellers, or between firms and employees.

What we *mean*, in ordinary usage, by 'unemployment' is exactly disruptions in, or difficulties in forming, employer–employee relationships. Simply hamstringing the auctioneer in a Walrasian framework that assigns no role at all to such a relationship is not going to give us the understanding we want. If we are serious about obtaining a theory of unemployment, we want a theory about unemployed *people*, not unemployed 'hours of labor services'; about people who look for jobs, hold them, lose them, people with all the attendant feelings that go along with these events. Walras's powerfully simple scenario, at least with the most obvious choice of 'commodity space', cannot give us this, with cleared markets or without them.[4]

A theory that does deal successfully with unemployment needs to address two quite distinct

4 Gary Hansen, 'Indivisible labour and the business cycle', and William Rogerson, 'Indivisible labour, lotteries, and the business cycle', use a commodity space in which agents trade 'lottery tickets' for hours supplied, so that one works a standard unit (say, 40 hours) with probability $1-\theta$ and not at all with probability θ. Here θ, which can be interpreted as an unemployment rate, is set in a competitive equilibrium. But in this set-up, as in fix-price models, there is no employer–employee relationship.

[53]

problems. One is the fact that job separations tend to take the form of unilateral decisions – a worker quits, or is laid off or fired – in which negotiations over wage rates play no explicit role. The second is that workers who lose jobs, for whatever reason, typically pass through a period of unemployment instead of taking temporary work on the 'spot' labor market jobs that are readily available in any economy. Of these, the second seems to me much the more important: it does not 'explain' why someone is unemployed to explain why he does not have a job with company *X*. After all, most employed people do not have jobs with company *X* either. To explain why people allocate time to a particular *activity* – like unemployment – we need to know why they prefer it to *all* other available activities: to say that I am allergic to strawberries does not 'explain' why I drink coffee. Neither of these puzzles is easy to understand within a Walrasian framework, and it would be good to understand both of them better, but I suggest we begin by focusing on the second of the two.

An analysis of unemployment as an *activity* was initiated by John McCall in a paper that integrated Stigler's ideas on the economics of search with the sequential analysis of Wald and Bellman.[5] McCall's

5 J. J. McCall, 'Economics of information and job search', *Quarterly Journal of Economics* **84** (February 1970), pp. 113–26; George J. Stigler, 'The economics of information', *Journal of Political Economy* **69** (June 1961), pp. 213–25;

contribution is well-known and justly celebrated, but I would like to celebrate it a little more, so I need to set out some details.

Consider an individual worker who begins a period with a job that pays him a wage w. He can either work a fixed number of hours, in which case he earns w, or search for another job, in which case he earns nothing and also loses the option to work at this wage later. If he works, the same wage w will be available to him next period with probability $1-\theta$; with probability θ he loses the job, beginning the next period with a wage of 0. Search is modeled as taking a drawing from a fixed probability distribution $G(w)$ of wage offers. The worker's objective is to maximize the expected present value of his earnings, discounted at the factor β.

Let $v(w)$ be the value of this objective for a worker who begins with the wage w and proceeds optimally. Then v must satisfy the Bellman equation:

$$v(w) = \max[w + \beta(1 - \theta)v(w) + \beta\theta v(0),$$
$$\beta \int v(w')dG(w')].$$

George J. Stigler, 'Information in the labor market', *Journal of Political Economy* **70** (October 1962), pp. 94–104; Abraham Wald, *Sequential Analysis* (Dover Publications, Inc., New York, 1973; 1st edn, John Wiley and Sons, 1947); Richard Bellman, *Dynamic Programming* (Princeton University Press, Princeton, 1957).

If the first term inside the brackets exceeds the second, the best decision is to work; if the second is larger, search is optimal.

The structure of this problem is well understood. There is a reservation wage $\bar{w}$, say, with the property that if $w \geqslant \bar{w}$ one works and if not, one searches. This reservation wage will be a function of the job-loss probability θ, the discount factor β, and the parameters of the offer-distribution G. The fraction of time this worker will spend searching, his long-run average unemployment rate, is given in terms of $\bar{w}$ by

$$u = \frac{\theta}{1 + \theta - G(\bar{w})}.$$

The theory also makes predictions about the duration of employment and unemployment spells, the earnings distribution of employed workers, and other aspects of the joint distribution of the time series on wage offers and actual earnings.

Here, then, is a prototype (at least) of a theory of unemployment. Let us take it seriously and criticize it. Indeed, the model's explicitness invites hard questioning. Why can the worker not work and search for alternative offers at the same time (the way economists do)? Doesn't he learn anything about his job opportunities as he searches? If he is no different from other workers, why does he face a distribution of wage possibilities (as

[56]

opposed to opportunities to work at 'the' going wage)?

These are all good questions, and we could think of more. Some of them are hard to deal with, some quite easy. But before turning to some of these questions, note this: in so criticizing McCall's model, we are *thinking* about unemployment, really thinking about what it is like to be unemployed in ways that fix-price and other macro-economic-level unemployment theories can never lead us to do. Questioning a McCall worker is like having a conversation with an out-of-work friend: 'Maybe you are setting your sights too high', or 'Why did you quit your old job before you had a new one lined up?' This is real social science: an attempt to model, to *understand*, human behavior by visualizing the situations people find themselves in, the options they face and the pros and cons as they themselves see them.

Among the questions raised about McCall's model of unemployment, the most pressing are those concerning its purely individual character. Granted that it is an interesting attempt to capture the decision problem faced by a worker *if* he were faced by a given distribution G of wage offers, what sort of world can we imagine that would place him in this situation? At one time, I thought this was a very hard question, but I now think it is an easy one to deal with, using the idea that Boyan Jovanovic introduced of jobs as 'matches' between

[57]

tasks and workers that are homogeneous in an *ex ante* sense but heterogeneous in an *ex post* sense.[6]

To be concrete, imagine a world in which all consumption consists of apples, grown on trees of varying heights. Though we could treat these trees as assets, and their owners as capitalists, let us keep the discussion simple for the moment and suppose that trees vastly outnumber people and so are priced at zero (with most apples simply rotting unpicked on their trees). To produce, a worker must be matched to a tree, with only one worker per tree. Like trees, workers come in varying heights, with tall workers best able to pick apples on tall trees (so they don't have to bend over) and short workers best on short trees. Let w now denote the number of apples a given worker can pick per period on a given tree, and let G denote the distribution of this random productivity. Finally, suppose that any given tree unpredictably becomes barren between one period and the next, with probability θ.

I would need to be a little more explicit about the nature of this imaginary world, except that I am sure you can see that what I am doing is simply inventing a 'technology' such that the Bellman equation of the McCall model holds for each individual agent, with w interpreted not as a

6 Boyan Jovanovic, 'Job matching and the theory of turnover', *Journal of Political Economy* **87** (December 1979), pp. 972–90.

market wage but as an idiosyncratic productivity variable. In so reinterpreting the McCall model as a simple general equilibrium system, let us give the worker preferences over sequences $\{c_t\}$ of consumption of the form:

$$E\left\{\sum_{t=0}^{\infty} \beta^t U(c_t)\right\}.$$

Then if each worker simply consumes his own real earnings w_t each period, the Bellman equation becomes:

$$v(w) = \max[U(w) + \beta(1 - \theta)v(w) + \beta\theta v(0),$$

$$U(0) + \beta\int v(w')dG(w')].$$

The structure of the problem remains as before, though of course the solution function v to the Bellman equation and the value $\bar{w}$ of the reservation wage will be different, and both will depend on the shape of the utility function U.

We have thus found one way to deal with the question: why do workers face a *distribution* of wage offers? This resolution does not violate the 'law of one price'. It simply rests on capturing in a tractable way the idea that different people are good at different things, and it can take some time and effort to find a task one is good at.

The general equilibrium in this McCall economy is one of autarchy: workers do not have to deal with capitalists since capital (trees) is so abundant that it is not worthwhile to establish property rights in it; neither do they trade with each other, since all any of them obtain from their labor is the single good: apples. As we start to complicate the model in various ways, however, matters quickly become much more interesting.

Though no one has any motive for spot trading, there is ample reason for workers to be interested in trading contingent claims on future goods. Each worker in the autarchic equilibrium bears the risk that the job he holds may vanish, and also the risk, once he is in the position of seeking a new job, that his search will turn up a string of bad matches. Suppose, at one extreme, that there is a continuum of these workers and that the situation of each of them, at each moment, is a matter of public knowledge. Under these circumstances workers will enter into pooling arrangements that smooth the consumption of each *perfectly,* requiring each member of the arrangement to take his work/ search decisions so as to maximize the market *value* of his earnings. This reinstates exactly the original McCall–Bellman equation, not because agents are risk-neutral, but because none has any risk to bear!

The pooling of earnings-risk predicted by this model is not at all what we observe. Consumption of similarly skilled workers is not at all well correlated and certainly varies with employment status. Moreover workers in occupations with high earnings variability command a premium that would not exist in a perfectly-insured environment. We used to label this situation as one of 'imperfect capital markets' and leave it at that, but simply giving an unsuccessful theory a high-sounding label does not produce a better theory. It has proved more fruitful to ask *why* these obviously useful earnings-insurance markets are not present in reality, as they are in the model.

The most interesting recent work focuses on the informational assumptions of this model, on its key assumption that each worker's situation is 'common knowledge'. Suppose, at the other extreme, that each worker's w is visible only to himself. Then a worker would be free both to claim a low wage offer and the insurance payment to which this would entitle him and to work secretly to acquire still more consumption. Clearly no complete private insurance scheme can survive this possibility.

This observation might suggest that the privacy of earnings information would leave only autarchy as an 'incentive compatible' equilibrium, but this is not the case if workers are able to build up a record by first putting in premiums and then obtaining benefits. The possible equilibrium arrangements for insurance, or for contingent borrowing and lending, under competitive conditions, in even so apparently simple a model as this, are only beginning to be explored, in work by Robert Townsend, Edward Green, Truman Bewley, Jose Scheinkman, Laurence Weiss, and

[61]

others.[7] It is not at all clear at this stage what assumptions about information (there are clearly many possibilities intermediate to the two extremes I have mentioned) will prove both tractable and consistent with the evidence we have on actual risk-sharing arrangements.

Since it is evident that, with private information, competitively determined arrangements will fall short of complete pooling, this class of models also raises the issue of *social insurance:* pooling arrangements that are not actuarially sound, and hence require support from compulsory taxation. The main elements of Kenneth Arrow's analysis of medical insurance are readily transferable to this employment context.[8] Recent, very interesting work by James Albrecht and Bo Axell contains more specific developments.[9]

7 Robert M. Townsend, 'Optimal multiperiod contracts and the gain from enduring relationships under private information', *Journal of Political Economy* **90,** 6 (December 1982), pp. 1166–87; Edward J. Green, 'Lending and the smoothing of uninsurable income', unpublished working paper, Board of Governors of the Federal Reserve System, 1985; Truman Bewley, 'Fiscal and Monetary Policy in a General Equilibrium Model', unpublished Cowles Foundation Discussion Paper No. 690, 1984; Jose A. Scheinkman and Laurence Weiss, 'Borrowing constraints and aggregate economic activity', *Econometrica* **54** (1986), pp. 23–45.
8 Kenneth J. Arrow, 'Welfare analysis of changes in health coinsurance rates', in Richard N. Rosett (ed.), *The Role of Health Insurance in the Health Services Sector* (NBER, New York, 1976).

[62]

A different set of problems is raised by this same model if we move away from the assumption that capital is a free good, and take these earnings opportunities – these 'trees' – to be owned by capitalists whose permission is required if they are to be utilized. For consider a worker who, after forgoing earnings opportunities elsewhere to engage in a job search, has located a tree that is an exceptionally good match, w, one that is recognized as such by the owner of the tree. The owner will surely reason that since the worker would have been willing to stay and work for anything above the reservation wage, he can charge the difference between w and that wage as 'rent'. But the worker understands that, should he leave, the next searcher to arrive will not likely be so well matched and, in any case, current earnings will be zero unless he accepts the position now. The situation has a lot of possibilities, and they are interesting possibilities because they resemble those we see in actual bargaining situations, but in a setting simple enough that some real analysis may be possible.

The situation may be described as one in which the worker and the owner have jointly acquired a piece of what Vincent Crawford has called

9 James W. Albrecht and Bo Axell, 'An equilibrium model of search unemployment', *Journal of Political Economy* **92** No. 5 (October 1984), pp. 824–40.

'relationship-specific capital'.[10] In my example, this capital came into existence at the pair's first meeting, so there was no possibility for advance arrangements for dealing with it. If such capital is accumulated more gradually, with the possibility of doing so anticipated by the two parties, it is clear that they both have an interest in dealing with this possibility in advance, or of deciding how the rent from a good match (should it be found) will be divided *before* either has made any commitment, at a time when both parties have other relatively attractive options. This advance division of yet-to-be-accumulated rents is, of course, exactly the point of contracts and, more generally, of business and individual reputations that form the basis of what Costas Azariadis called 'implicit' contracts.[11]

As with the study of information-based limitations on private insurance or credit possibilities,

10 Vincent P. Crawford, 'Long-term relationships governed by short-term contracts', Industrial Relations Section, Princeton University, Working Paper No. 205, Princeton, 1986.
11 Costas Azariadis, 'Implicit contracts and underemployment equilibria', *Journal of Political Economy* **83** (1975), pp. 1183–202. This paper and the related one by Martin N. Baily, 'Wages and employment under uncertain demand', *Review of Economic Studies* **41** (1974), pp. 37–50, have given rise to an enormous literature. A valuable recent survey is provided by Sherwin Rosen, 'Implicit contracts: a survey', *Journal of Economic Literature* **23** (September 1985), pp. 1133–173.

the study of labor contracts, explicit or implicit, can take many directions, depending on which aspects one wishes to use simplifying assumptions to emphasize. As this theory evolves, it may well turn out to open up new possibilities (relative to those considered by Kydland and Prescott) for the way the economy responds to outside shocks. This is the line pursued, for example, in a recent paper by Scheinkman and Weiss in which the private sector's response to technology shocks is fundamentally altered by the absence of markets in which technological risks can be pooled.[12]

The developments in these two related lines of research would make a marvelous subject for some future set of lectures, but from the point of view of my present purposes, they are a digression that has perhaps already grown too lengthy. I wish to conclude with two general observations.

I have centered this discussion of unemployment on McCall's original model of the decision problem facing a single unemployed worker. As soon as this simple problem is *stated*, it leads to a host of questions about this worker's objectives and his market opportunities, which in turn leads directly to some of the central questions of the theory of unemployment: 'What are the arrangements that market economies have for allocating individual workers to specific tasks?'; 'What

12 Scheinkman and Weiss, 'Borrowing constraints'.

arrangements are available to allocate earnings and employment risks?'; and 'What are the possibilities for improving on these arrangements through social insurance and other policies?' McCall's decision to model unemployment as 'voluntary' (given the situation in which the worker finds himself) was, and still is, subjected to ignorant political criticism, as though it implied an attitude of public indifference toward unemployment. In fact, as we have seen, it is exactly this 'voluntary' aspect of McCall's formulation that leads it immediately into the first coherent analysis of employment-related risks and to a sharp identification of exactly why it is that private markets deal inadequately with these risks and what forms of public policy can hope to alleviate them.

It is a remarkable and, I think, instructive fact that in nearly 50 years the Keynesian tradition has produced not one useful model of the individual unemployed worker, and no rationale for unemployment insurance beyond the observation that, in common with countercyclical cash grants to corporations or to anyone else, it has the effect of increasing the total volume of spending at the right times. By dogmatically insisting that unemployment be classed as 'involuntary' this tradition simply cut itself off from serious thinking about the actual options unemployed people are faced with, and hence from learning anything about how alternative social arrangements might improve these options.[13]

[66]

In my view, focusing on unemployment as an *individual* problem, identical in character in business cycle peaks and troughs (though more people have this problem in troughs) is the key step in designing social policies to deal with it. But I began this section with another question in mind as well: whether modeling *aggregative* employment in a competitive way as in the Kydland and Prescott model (and hence lumping unemployment together with 'leisure' and all other non-work activities) is a serious strategic error in trying to account for business cycles. I see no reason to believe that it is. If the hours people work – *choose* to work – are fluctuating it is because they are substituting into some other activity. For some purposes – designing an unemployment com-

13 In some of the models alluded to in this section, equilibria can have features described, without too much strain, as 'involuntary unemployment'. For example, a worker who chooses to enter a 'lottery' that determines his employment status and ends up not working could be called 'involuntarily' unemployed (although in the Hansen and Rogerson papers, such workers are happier than those who draw employment!). In some contract models, the employer designates which workers will not work in particular (privately observed) circumstances. Some writers describe such equilibria as 'Keynesian' (with an eye toward their own future employment status?) but none of these equilibria even *suggests* the existence of 'slack' or 'deadweight losses' in the economy that can be removed by policies that affect the aggregate volume of spending.

[67]

pensation scheme, for example – it will clearly be essential to break non-work hours into finer categories, including as one 'activity' unemployment. But such a finer breakdown need not substantially alter the problem Kydland and Prescott have tried to face of finding a parameterization of preferences over goods and hours that is consistent with observed employment movements.

Neither do I think that improvements in our understanding of labor contracts are likely to alter by much our explanations of employment fluctuations. What these theories *do* promise, and this is important, is a more satisfactory account of the nature of job separations and in particular of the widespread use by firms of non-wage rationing in reducing the workforce. Assuming a given job-loss probability θ, as I did in my exposition of McCall's model, is clearly not an explanation for this practice. But however well we succeed in accounting for separations we will still be left with the problem of understanding the behavior of individual workers once they are separated, and of explaining why they react to this situation – *choose* to react to it – by substituting against work.

Static models of labor contracting do not even make a beginning on this question and neither, I conjecture, will dynamic versions. Some of them do, however, predict average or 'natural' unemployment rates that exceed efficient rates, or predict that people will devote too much time to the activity 'unemployment'. This raises the possibility that welfare improvements can be obtained by taxing this activity in a uniform way over time. One cannot rule out this possibility in principle (though my own guess would be that on balance, efficiency requires subsidizing unemployment and hence increasing its average level), but with respect to questions of stabilization policy, this is obviously a side issue.

VI

Nominal variables – the quantity of money, the general price level, and nominal rates of interest – play no role in the Kydland–Prescott model, nor do these variables figure in the large volume of recent research that examines the reasons for and consequences of various non-competitive contracting arrangements. One consequence of this omission is that these theories cannot shed light on the problem of inflation or on the observed associations between movements in money and prices and real economic activity. It is far from self-evident that these omissions are deficiencies: it is easy enough to graft monetary complications onto a real model, with the money supply responding to real events but playing no causal role, in such a way as to match the co-movements we observe and to provide a monetary account of movements in other nominal variables. In a moment, I will outline one model that does just this, and perhaps this is all the monetary theory we need.

But I do not believe that this is the case. Our attention is drawn to the evidence Friedman and Schwartz and others have assembled associating monetary contractions with depressions in real activity, not because this evidence documents an independent 'causal' role for money, but because these real movements appear to be too large to be induced by a combination of purely real shocks and the kind of 'propagation mechanism' Kydland–Prescott constructed.[1] To account for depressions of the magnitude of those observed in the 1870–1940 period (and, I think, for more recent recessions as well) we need *either* much larger shocks than any that can be interpreted as 'technology' shocks in a Kydland–Prescott framework, *or* a propagation mechanism with much larger 'multipliers'. The problem is not the difficulty of constructing theories that account for the Friedman–Schwartz evidence with passively responding money – this is easy to do. It lies in accounting for large real fluctuations without candidates for 'shocks' that are of the right order of magnitude.

1 Milton Friedman and Anna J. Schwartz, *A Monetary History of the United States, 1867–1960*, National Bureau of Economic Research Monograph (Princeton University Press, Princeton, 1963, and *Monetary Trends in the United States and the United Kingdom*, National Bureau of Economic Research Monograph (The University of Chicago Press, Chicago, 1982).

[71]

(This is not a question Kydland and Prescott deal with in their paper, for they simply choose the variance of the technology shock so as to be consistent with observed GNP variability. This is not one of the parameters on which they provide independent evidence. Such evidence is, in principle, obtainable, using Solow's method for estimating 'technical change' (defined exactly as Kydland and Prescott do) from time series on output, inputs and factor shares. There would be difficulties in interpreting cyclical movements in technical change, so measured, as 'pure' technology shocks (due to fluctuations in capital utilization), but even if one were willing to interpret them in this way, I do not believe they would be variable enough to do *all* the work in explaining output variability. This is an empirical question that merits more work.)[2]

What I would like to do next, then, is to introduce money into a neoclassical dynamic framework in such a way as to restate in modern terms the quantity theory of money, inflation and interest. This will be of interest in its own right, and it will also permit us to arrive at a theoretical statement of what the problem of accounting for money-induced depressions seems to involve. At this stage of our knowledge, a clear statement of

2 On this issue, see Edward C. Prescott, 'Theory ahead of business cycle measurement', Carnegie–Rochester Conference paper, 1985.

the problem may be all we can hope for, but I will postpone consideration of this question until we have such a statement in front of us.

Money has value in exchange but not in use, so to think about money we need to think about exchange – how it takes place, and what about its character gives money its value. In a real general equilibrium model like Kydland and Prescott's, exchange occurs in centralized markets, so that goods are valued only if they are valued in use (consumption or production) by someone. To model a monetary economy, one thus needs to imagine that trading is decentralized in some way. My preference is to do this in a way that does minimal violence to the original, real theory that is being modified, so as not to discard altogether the theory's considerable ability to account for important real observations, but this is an imprecise criterion at best. In any case, here is a specific example.

Think of trade in securities – a full range of Arrow–Debreu contingent claims, together with fiat currency and contingent claims on future currency – as occurring at the *beginning* of each trading day, say 9.00–9.15 a.m. After securities trading is concluded, production and exchange of current goods is carried out in the remainder of the day, in what I want to think of as a decentralized fashion. By 'decentralized' I mean firms that are spatially scattered, with workers selling labor to a particular firm, going to a specific location to do so, losing contact with other buyers of labor, and shoppers purchasing goods from a particular firm similarly obliged to go to its specific location. In so far as goods and labor have been contracted for in advance, evidence of such contracts is simply presented by buyers and/or sellers at each location, with the indicated exchange then taking place. Equivalently, under rational expectations, one may think of sellers in these transactions issuing invoices, or trade credit, to be cleared at tomorrow's securities market. In either case, the relevant price and quantity determination is made in the competitive securities market, with only the actual execution of trades taking place elsewhere.

In a complete-markets model such as Kydland and Prescott's, *all* exchange can be thought of as being executed in this way, so that while one may want to think of economic activities like producing and consuming as occurring in a decentralized way, nothing is lost, and much analytical simplicity is gained, by thinking of all economic *decisions* as arrived at in a single, centralized market. Here, to motivate the use of money, a subset of consumption goods – 'cash goods' – will be thought of as exchanged in circumstances where the buyer is unknown to the seller, so that the latter is unwilling either to accept as payment claims issued in earlier securities trading or to issue trade credit to be discharged later. Such goods, if purchased at all, *must* be paid for with currency acquired in advance: at the securities market of that morning, or earlier.[3]

[74]

This simple setting permits a unified treatment of both the portfolio and the transactions (or inventory-theoretic) aspects of individual money demand, and does so in a way that permits the calculation of a monetary general equilibrium. When engaged in securities trading, an agent allocates a given amount of perfectly fungible wealth among cash and other securities. To determine the return on cash relevant for solving this

---

3 The model sketched here is a variation on that introduced in Robert E. Lucas, Jr and Nancy L. Stokey, 'Optimal fiscal and monetary policy in an economy without capital', *Journal of Monetary Economics* **12** (1983), pp. 55–93, and analyzed in more detail in Robert E. Lucas, Jr and Nancy L. Stokey, 'Money and interest in a cash-in-advance economy', *Econometrica* (forthcoming). Scenarios that help to motivate the Clower-constraint are provided in Peter W. Howitt, 'Stability and the quantity theory', *Journal of Political Economy* **82** (1974), pp. 133–51; Robert E. Lucas, Jr, 'Equilibrium in a pure currency economy', *Economic Inquiry* **18** (1980), pp. 203–20; and Robert M. Townsend, 'Asset-return anomalies in a monetary economy', *Journal of Economic Theory* (forthcoming). The basic convention was proposed in D. H. Robertson, 'Saving and Hoarding', reprinted in *Essays in Monetary Theory* (P. S. King and Son, London, 1940); S. C. Tsiang, 'Liquidity preferences and loanable funds theories, multiplier and velocity analysis: a synthesis', *American Economic Review* **46** (1956), pp. 540–64; and Robert W. Clower, 'A reconsideration of the microfoundations of monetary theory', *Western Economic Journal* **6** (1967), pp. 1–9. See Meir Kohn, 'In Defense of the Finance Constraint', Dartmouth College Working Paper, 1980, for a useful intellectual history and related discussion.

portfolio problem, the agent looks forward to the fact that he will soon be in a different trading situation, where assets are not perfectly fungible, where cash can be used to effect certain exchanges that other securities cannot.

When engaged in goods trading, the agent similarly looks forward to the fact that cash inventories carried over can be traded on future securities markets. In both cases, the way money is valued in any given trading situation depends on its anticipated value in subsequent, perhaps quite different, trading situations. By postulating an individual with specific preferences over cash and credit goods, and by being specific as well about the timing with which information gets revealed, we can derive all of classical monetary theory by just thinking through the margins on which an agent operates in this world of centralized/decentralized markets. Let me do this next.

Let current period utility be a function $U(c_{1t}, c_{2t})$ of the amounts of cash goods c_{1t} and credit goods c_{2t} consumed in t. Let r_t be the nominal interest rate set in securities trading at the beginning of t, and assume that all period t information is revealed at the beginning (so that an agent receives no surprises in the course of trading for goods). In this situation, agents will conclude securities trading holding *exactly* the 'real balances' $m_t = M_t/P_t$ needed to finance their intended purchases c_{1t} of cash goods later in the period, putting the rest of their wealth in bonds bearing the

[76]

interest return r_t or in other income-yielding securities. Planned purchases of credit goods do not require this holding of assets in the form of cash, since these invoices can be discharged later (by selling bonds, for example). Hence the relative price of cash and credit goods is just $1 + r_t$, and the marginal condition

$$1 + r_t = \frac{U_1(c_{1t}, c_{2t})}{U_2(c_{1t}, c_{2t})} \tag{11}$$

must obtain in an equilibrium.

There is a second, intertemporal, margin that also bears on an agent's cash-holding decision. Picture the agent now engaged in goods trading, with an option of acquiring one additional dollar's worth of credit goods. Doing so yields utility, on the margin, of $(1/P_t)U_2(c_{1t}, c_{2t})$. On the other hand, this will give him one less dollar for spending on cash goods next period, at a cost in terms of current utility of $\beta(1/P_{t+1})U_1(c_{1,t+1}, c_{2,t+1})$. Since this second cost is uncertain as of date t, we obtain the marginal condition:

$$\frac{1}{P_t}U_2(c_{1t}, c_{2t}) = \beta E_t\left\{\frac{1}{P_{t+1}}U_1(c_{1,t+1}, c_{2,t+1})\right\}. \tag{12}$$

Isn't it curious that the rate of interest appears in the contemporaneous marginal condition (11) and not in the intertemporal one, (12)? We are used to

[77]

thinking of securities as *the* way of moving purchasing power across time, so we expect to see a securities yield in conditions like (12).[4] But it is central to monetary theory that there are intertemporal movements in purchasing power that cannot be effected with securities: otherwise, we wouldn't need the money! There is no monetary theory that does not have a condition like (12) in it somewhere; I am only being a little more explicit about it than is customary.

Everything that is valid in the traditional quantity theory of money can be extracted from these two marginal conditions, as can much that is new. Since cash balances are spent entirely on cash goods, real balances are given by $m_t = c_{1t}$ and $c_{2t} = c_t - m_t$, where c_t is total consumption. With these changes of variables, (11) reads:

$$1 + r_t = \frac{U_1(m_t, c_t - m_t)}{U_2(m_t, c_t - m_t)}. \tag{13}$$

Equations (11) and (12), combined and rearranged, yield:

$$\frac{1}{1 + r_t} = \beta E_t \left\{ \frac{P_t}{P_{t+1}} \cdot \frac{U_1(m_{t+1}, c_{t+1} - m_{t+1})}{U_1(m_t, c_t - m_t)} \right\} \tag{14}$$

Now equation (13) relates the three variables: real balances, total real consumption spending, and the

4 Of course, the interest rate can be reintroduced into (12) by substituting for $U_2(c_{1t}, c_{2t})$ from (11).

nominal interest rate. We can think of it as a conventional demand function for real balances, in implicit form. Equation (13) expresses the price $(1 + r_t)^{-1}$ of a nominal bond as the product of two terms: $(P_t/P_{t+1}) = (1/1 + \pi_{t+1})$, where π_{t+1} is the inflation rate between this period and the next, and the marginal rate of substitution, $\beta(U_1(t+1)/U_1(t))$. Since neither of these factors is known as of date t, the formula involves the expectation $E_t(\cdot)$, conditioned on date-t information. In this trading context, then, we can derive the money demand function *and* Irving Fisher's decomposition of the interest rate into a 'real' rate and an 'inflation premium' – that is to say, we can derive all of the implications of the quantity theory of money – from straightforward considerations of utility theory. Moreover, this derivation does not depend in any way on assumptions about the nature of monetary or real shocks impinging on the system.

Now equations (13) and (14) are components of a general equilibrium system of a monetary economy (just as the quantity theory and the Fisher equation are) but it is not clear what they imply for behavior until the rest of the system is filled in. The simplest way to do this is to take *both* total consumption c_t and the rate of growth of the money supply M_t/M_{t-1} as exogenously given, in which case (13) and (14) become a theory of the determination of the price level and the interest rate. To be concrete, let s_t denote the 'state of the

[79]

system' at date t, assumed known to all agents as of the beginning of t, and assume that $\{s_t\}$ follows a Markov process with transitions given by:

$$\pi(s', s)ds' = Pr\{s_{t+1} \in [s', s' + ds'] \mid s_t = s\}.$$

Let c_t be a fixed function $y(s_t)$ of s_t, and let $M_t/M_{t-1} = g(s_t)$, also a fixed function. (Here one could think of the state s_t as being the pair $(c_t, (M_t/M_{t-1}))$, but s_t might well include other, purely informational variables as well.) Then analyzing this system means tracing out the way the behavior of the process $\{P_t, r_t\}$ responds to changes in π, y and g.

All the necessary ingredients for this analysis are at hand. It is easiest to begin with (12) and to view the 'unknown' in the system as a function $m(s_t)$ giving equilibrium real balances M_t/P_t as a function of the state s_t. Then since $\{M_t\}$ is an exogenous process, this will determine the path $\{P_t\}$ of the price level. Having done this, we can recover the path $\{r_t\}$ of interest rates from (13) (or, equivalently, from (14)). Multiplying (12) through by M_t, we have:

$$\frac{M_t}{P_t} U_2\left(\frac{M_t}{P_t}, c_t - \frac{M_t}{P_t}\right)$$

$$= \beta E_t\left\{\frac{M_{t+1}}{P_{t+1}} \cdot \frac{M_t}{M_{t+1}} U_1\left(\frac{M_{t+1}}{P_{t+1}}, c_{t+1} - \frac{M_{t+1}}{P_{t+1}}\right)\right\}.$$

Given our assumptions about the evolution of the variables c_t and M_t, this can be restated more usefully as:

[80]

$$m(s)U_2(m(s), y(s) - m(s))$$

$$= \beta \int \frac{m(s')}{g(s')} U_1(m(s'), c(s') - m(s'))\pi(s', s)ds'.$$
(15)

Equation (15) is a single equation in the unknown function $m(s)$, given the functions π, y and g. A relatively complete analysis of this functional equation is given in a recent paper by Nancy Stokey and myself,[5] but for present purposes it will suffice to point out certain properties that a solution function $m(s)$ must have, and work out an example or two.

Let us first locate the neutrality theorem – *any* serious monetary model must have one of these, of course. If $m(s)$ solves (15) and an initial money supply M_0 is given, then

$$P_0 = \frac{M_0}{m(s_0)}, P_1 = \frac{M_1}{m(s_1)} = M_0 \frac{g(s_1)}{m(s_1)},$$

and in general:

$$P_t = M_0 \frac{g(s_1) \dots g(s_t)}{m(s_t)}$$

describes the equilibrium price path. Hence multiplying the initial money stock by some $\lambda > 0$

5 Lucas and Stokey, 'Money and interest'.

and *leaving the system otherwise unchanged* has the effect of multiplying the price level by this same factor λ, now and for all future dates. Since $m(s_t)$ is unaffected, so too will be $c_t = (m(s_t), g(s_t) - m(s_t))$. I should think we would view any monetary model that did *not* have this neutrality property with the deepest suspicions, the way we would view a physical model that predicted different times for the earth to complete its orbit depending on whether distance is measured in miles or kilometers.

This neutrality theorem does not say much about the way monetary shocks generated by the process (π, g) affect prices or the composition of consumption. For this, we need to study (15) in more detail. A key observation is that the current state s appears on the right hand side of (15) only as it enters into the transition density $\pi(s', s)$, or *only* as s_t provides information useful in forecasting future states $s_{t+1}, s_{t+2}, \ldots$. To see what this means, consider the case of serially independent shocks, so that $\pi(s', s)$ depends only on s', and the current shock s_t gives *no* information about the future. Then the right side of (15) is constant with respect to s (call its value A, say), and we can solve for real balances $m(s_t)$ as a fixed function of $c_t = y(s_t)$ and A. Here is *another* neutrality theorem, quite different in character from the first. It says that given the output realizations $\{c_t\}$, all movements in M_t – not just once-and-for-all movements – are immediately reflected in equipro-

[82]

portional movements in the price level, and have no effects on resource allocation. In other words, only anticipated money shocks matter. Unanticipated shocks to money are neutral. Money has real effects in this model only if it affects one of the margins (13) or (14). It can affect (13) only through affecting nominal interest r_t and from (14), it can affect r_t only by affecting expectations about future equilibria.

As soon as we get away from serial independence, of course, such expectations effects become the rule, and this strong neutrality theorem is 'lost'. The case of logarithmic utility gives some of the flavor of the general situation. Let $U(c_1, c_2) = \alpha \ln(c_1) + \ln(c_2)$ so that $c_1 U_1(c_1, c_2) = \alpha$ and (15) reduces to

$$\frac{m(s)}{y(s) - m(s)} = \alpha\beta \int \frac{1}{g(s')} \pi(s', s)ds'. \tag{16}$$

The term $\int (1/g(s')) \pi(s', s)ds'$ is just the expected *decline* in the money supply, M_t/M_{t+1}, expressed as a function of current information s: call it $B(s)$. Then we can solve (16) for real balances

$$\frac{M_t}{P_t} = m(s_t) = \left\{ 1 + \frac{1}{\alpha\beta B(s_t)} \right\}^{-1} y(s_t)$$

so that the function $1 + 1/(\alpha\beta B(s_t))$ is just equilibrium *velocity*. Using (13), together with (16), the

[83]

one-period nominal bond price is

$$\frac{1}{1+r_t} = \alpha^{-1}\frac{m_t}{c_t - m_t} = \beta B(s_t). \tag{17}$$

In general, then, both interest rates and prices will fluctuate with the information that current variables s_t convey about future monetary movements. Does a monetary expansion – a high realization of the random variable $g(s_t) = (M_t/M_{t-1})$ – drive bond prices up or down? Economic theory – at least, *this* economic theory – is silent on this point. The answer, from (17), depends on the function $B(s_t)$ that describes the way the monetary authority reacts to current and past shocks, and anything is economically possible. This does not mean, however, that the theory is vacuous: though it does not restrict individual correlations, it does place restrictions on the relationship between the given *functions $B(s)$* and *y(s)* and the endogenously-determined equilibrium functions $m(s)$ and $r(s)$.

In summary, models of the type described in this section can reproduce standard quantity-theoretic results and also capture certain effects of erratic monetary policies on resource allocations. Whether these monetary non-neutralities form a sufficient basis on which to construct a monetary theory of business cycles remains to be seen.

VII

The integration of monetary elements of the sort I have been discussing with the kind of real dynamics captured in the Kydland and Prescott model is, at present, slightly beyond the frontier of what is technically possible. But, reasoning by analogy from what is known from related, existing work, we can, I think, arrive at some useful conjectures as to how such a hybrid model would behave. Of the possibilities available to us, I think this is the best way we have of thinking about a monetary business cycle.

To be specific about the hybrid model I have in mind, let preferences and the technology for producing goods be exactly as in Kydland and Prescott. Let trading, on the other hand, follow the alternating pattern I have used to motivate the use of money, with agents trading in securities at the beginning of a period and then using cash acquired in the course of this trading to buy some of their consumption goods later on in the period. Let us treat labor as a credit good, so that workers are paid at the end of a period, and investment goods as credit goods as well. Then the two marginal conditions I derived earlier for a monetary economy continue to hold in an equilibrium, except that the consumption of leisure will appear as an argument of the marginal utility functions as well as the consumption of both kinds of goods. (Why would such a model be difficult to solve? I am not sure it would be, looked at in the right way, but it is clear that its solution cannot be obtained by solving a system-wide maximum problem as Kydland and Prescott solved their model. The introduction of money introduces a wedge of inefficiency that precludes this solution method.)

What I would like to do with this model is to postulate an erratic money supply, modeled as a stochastic process, the parameters of which remain fixed over time and known to agents. It makes no difference if these money movements react to movements in real variables or not: statistical exogeneity will play no role in the story. I want to ask, then, under what conditions will monetary expansions be associated with real expansions, expansions of the same character as those induced by favorable technology shocks in the Kydland and Prescott model, and when will monetary contractions be associated with contractions in real output and employment?

We need to know how these money fluctuations take place and what information people have about them. Assume, first, that they occur via

[86]

open-market operations in the course of securities trading, and that their magnitude is always a matter of public knowledge as they occur. Under these circumstances, it should be clear from the discussion in the last section that the *direct* effect of a change in money is a pure units change. In so far as the change does not convey information about the way money or other variables will change in the future, it will simply induce a proportional response in all nominal prices – securities and goods – and have no effect on relative prices or other real magnitudes. In general, however, a change in money will convey information about future changes (depending on the nature of the stochastic process money follows), and it is these anticipation effects that have to account for any real response that does occur. It is *only* anticipated changes in money that matter, in this context.

How do these anticipation effects work? Suppose an event occurs that signals a monetary expansion between this period and the next. (Say, a monetary expansion currently in a situation where changes are positively autocorrelated, or equivalently, a monetary contraction currently in a situation of negative autocorrelation.) Then nominal interest will rise (these are simultaneous equations, so these 'chains' of effects are conjectural) and cash goods will become more expensive relative to credit goods, including leisure and investment goods. People will consume more leisure – employment will fall – and more credit

[87]

goods. The effect on investment could go either way. Basically, there is a rise in the 'inflation tax' and people will try to economize on money holdings by substituting against the activities that require its use. For a monetary contraction to induce a real contraction, then, it would have to set up anticipations of a subsequent expansion, inducing agents to cut back on cash-using activities like working and spending.

Now I know of no evidence to suggest that inflation tax effects of this type are negligible. These non-neutralities may well play a role in actual business cycles. It is, I suppose, exactly the fact that so much is going on at once that makes the empirical study of business cycles so difficult. But I find it difficult to believe that these effects can contribute very much to the explanation of major depressions or even of relatively minor post-war recessions. The predicted interest rate movements are in the wrong direction, and I do not see how effects of this type could stimulate the kind of investment response that plays such an important role in the propagation mechanism of Kydland and Prescott's model and in many earlier models.

I prefer to pursue the more conventional view that the real effects of monetary contractions arise by a very different route from the inflation tax effects we have been discussing, that they arise instead because a monetary contraction has real effects, not only through its *information effects*, but also through a *direct* effect, the latter arising

[88]

because nominal prices do not respond in proportion to movements in money as they occur. That is to say, I would like to consider the prospects for monetary business cycle models based on some kind of nominal price *rigidity*. Exactly because this point of departure is so widely shared, I had better be clear on what I mean by a *rigidity*, and about what would be required to incorporate such an effect in a useful economic model.

I use the term price rigidity to refer to a particular prediction error in classical models of the type I have just reviewed, situations in which the model predicts that a change in money will have a pure units effect, moving prices in proportion and quantities and relative prices not at all, but in which prices are observed to respond *less* than proportionally, and quantities similarly react 'inappropriately'. Conventional wisdom aside, the documenting of such an event is not so easy — the theory of the last section gives some idea of what would have to be 'controlled for' to do so. Certainly the term rigidity does *not* refer to some characteristic of nominal price or wage series by themselves, but rather to the behavior of these series relative to the way they would have been predicted to behave under a particular class of models. In any case, let us proceed under the assumption that price rigidities in this prediction error sense do occur, and ask what theoretical responses to this situation might take us somewhere. Obviously, if a model constructed under

[89]

certain assumptions makes predictions that con-
tradict fact, we need to review the assumptions and
change some of them.

The traditional response, of course, is simply to
add some form of price-rigidity to the model and
discard one of the original equilibrium conditions.
This is the resolution Franco Modigliani worked
out in his 1944 paper – discarding (in some range
of the variables) the labor supply function or the
assumption that labor markets 'clear' – and it is an
idea that continues to be refined in various ways.[1]
It seems clear that this resolution as it stands
cannot be reconciled with the theoretical viewpoint I proposed in section II: agents are assumed
to *think* they are playing a competitive game when
in fact the model assumes they are not. We used to
react to this situation by saying: 'Well, that's macroeconomics for you', but what is the point of simply
elevating our inability to model something sensibly
into a theoretical 'principle'?

Conditions of theoretical consistency aside, this
empirically motivated resolution doesn't *work*.
The problem with price rigidities is that they seem
to come and go. Sometimes monetary changes that
'ought' to be pure units effects seem to be just
that; sometimes they seem to have large non-
neutral effects. Macroeconomists have tried to
deal with this by proposing various taxonomies to
decide which theory to apply to which situation:

1 Franco Modigliani, 'Liquidity preference and the theory
of interest and money', *Econometrica* **12** (1944).

use the classical model when employment is 'full'; the rigid model otherwise. Use the classical model for 'long-run' situations, the rigid model for the 'short-run'. But no one has produced a set of useful criteria for deciding which of these situations the economy is in at any particular time, so such taxonomies provide little more than a system for labeling economic events after the fact. They are serving only to underscore the futility of theorizing by postulating that the behavior of agents is what it is without trying to locate the *reasons* for this behavior in preferences, technology, or the structure of the underlying game.

More recently, a number of writers have tried to trace the reasons for price rigidities back to the idea that agents sign nominally-denominated contracts for periods of up to several years, fixing wages and/or prices in advance. John Taylor, in particular, has constructed an operational econometric model in which prices are assumed to be set in this way.[2] More recently, Deborah Lucas has investigated a theoretical model in which it is taken as a part of the 'rules of the game' that some goods are contracted for in advance at competitively set (but thereafter, rigid) nominal prices.[3] In Lucas's

2 Taylor, 'Estimation and control of a macroeconomic model'.
3 Deborah J. Lucas, 'Price and interest rate dynamics induced by multiperiod contracts in a cash-in-advance economy', unpublished University of Chicago working paper, 1984.

[91]

model, agents are assumed to solve well-specified maximum problems, so that the system is in a genuine equilibrium in the sense of section II. Both models have the property that a change in money that 'ought', classically, to have pure units effects only does so asymptotically, but quite complicated non-neutral dynamic responses occur in the meantime. These models succeed in making explicit the idea that 'long-run' neutrality can be combined with 'short-run' rigidity, and Taylor's evidence for the US economy indicates some empirical promise for this way of unifying classical and fix-price theories. Moreover, as Taylor has rightly observed, we have a great deal of independent evidence on contracting practices, so that particular macro-economically-useful assumptions can be checked in the same way that, say, assumed gestation lags in Kydland and Prescott's model can be, and in a way that auctioneer behavior in other fix-price models cannot be.

It has frequently been suggested that models of this type have some connection with theories of equilibrium-contracting, of the type I alluded to in my discussion of unemployment theory, a possibility that Milton Harris and Bengt Holmstrom have explored in a recent paper.[4] But, as Harris and Holmstrom observed, the central idea of

4 Milton Harris and Bengt Holmstrom, 'Microeconomic developments and macroeconomics', *American Economic Review* 73 (1983), pp. 223–7.

modern contract theory is to use the assumption that agents have valuable, *private* information to rationalize the existence and form of observed contracts. In Taylor's and Lucas's formulations, and in all other macroeconomic applications (loosely speaking) of contract theory of which I am aware, *all* information is assumed to be public – exactly as it is in Kydland and Prescott or in the monetary model I sketched in the last section. The reason unanticipated money shocks are neutral (information or inflation tax effects aside) in the monetary model of section VI, is that changes in money are assumed to be known to all agents as soon as they occur, and can therefore be immediately 'corrected for'. If *this* assumption is retained, then even in a world with fairly complicated contractual arrangements the same 'correction' will simply be built into equilibrium contracts. Of course, if the assumption that monetary movements are public information as soon as they occur is dropped, new and interesting possibilities *do* arise. I shall return to this later on.

The idea that the theory of contracts will provide a new rationale for *nominal* price rigidity, or for monetary non-neutralities in addition to inflation taxes, is similar to the older idea that monopolistic elements can play the same theoretical role. The underlying idea is the not-unreasonable one that since money can often be shown in competitive theoretical models to possess neutrality properties that do not seem to obtain in reality, replacing the assumption of *competition* with some other assumed form of interaction will yield theories that are closer to reality with respect to their predictions about money and prices. The conjecture has the rhetorical advantage that it is difficult to check, since theories of non-competitive games are in a state of relative infancy. But it overlooks the *triviality* of the standard monetary neutrality theorems, and hence their insensitivity to the nature of the equilibrium being studied. The theory of monopoly, competently worked out, assigns no role to monetary units, and one is free to normalize prices in equilibria with monopoly elements exactly as one can in competitive equilibria. Results on the *existence* of equilibria with imperfect competition are indeed much harder to establish than existence results under competition, but neutrality theorems take the form 'if an equilibrium exists it has the following property', and their proofs take the form of showing that multiplying *nominal* equilibrium magnitudes by a common positive number yields another equilibrium. Results like this are not special to *competitive* equilibria, and nothing in the modern theory of contracts or of other non-competitive games suggests that they are.

The central issue for a theory of nominal price rigidity, it seems to me, is not the nature of the game agents are assumed to be engaged in, but rather the *information* agents are assumed to have about the state of the system at each date. In so far

[94]

as the monetary information necessary to permit agents to correct for what are, or ought to be, units changes is public (either directly or because it is 'revealed' through movements in prices or other variables), then one would expect this information to be used, independent of the form of interaction among agents. If, on the other hand, this information is *not* public, this simple 'correction' will not be possible and other possibilities present themselves. I think the construction of a satisfactory theory of a money-induced business cycle must involve exploiting these possibilities in some way.

Let me come back to the decision problem faced by firms and households in the Kydland and Prescott model, with emphasis on the information these agents have and on how they interpret it. Agents begin a period with the history of past inputs and outputs from the production process, which gives them some information on the 'technology' they have now and will have in the future. In addition they obtain, in some direct way, an advance 'signal' on current technical change, and on the basis of this they decide on current inputs and on new investment projects to be initiated. Production takes place, and this gives more technological information on the basis of which the division of production into sales and inventory accumulation is determined. (Of course, price movements mediate between firms and consumers as these quantity decisions are made.) The information in this scenario is entirely about

[95]

technology, in the sense of output per unit of inputs, and it is entirely public. As Kydland and Prescott showed, if the technology shocks are large enough, these responses to them produce business cycle-like dynamics.

Now imagine a system with many different goods, each with its own stochastic process for technological change, so that the decision problem I have described involves distributing hours of employment across the production of different goods, as well as a work–'leisure' decision, and so that many different kinds of investment projects are possible. These *individual* technology shocks will be much more variable than the index numbers that play this role at the aggregative level, and future values will be much less predictable. We know from index number theory that there is no hope that such a model would aggregate *perfectly* to the model Kydland and Prescott studied, but we have much experience suggesting that it would come fairly close, and of course this is the way we interpret a 'single-good' model of any kind.

In such a many-good elaboration of the model, shifts in the composition of product demand would be modeled in a way very similar to the way Kydland and Prescott model technology shifts, viewed either as shifts in tastes or as the introduction of new goods providing consumers with different mixes of 'characteristics' from those provided by the old goods. From the point of view of producers, a new-found ability to make *more* widgets with given inputs comes to very much the same thing as the ability to produce widgets that people *like* better than the old ones. Again, I think elaborations in this direction, if they could be carried out, would lead to dynamic behavior of aggregates very similar to Kydland and Prescott's, and for the same reasons as in their model.

In imagining these elaborations, I am retaining the assumption that all information is public, but the *volume* of such information is exploding: we are now thinking of *millions* of bits of new information on tastes and technology becoming available each period. Each 'bit' may be easy, even free, to acquire, but with any kind of cost associated with processing this information, people are going to economize, processing only those observations that materially sharpen their ability to make their own production and investment decisions well. If we were to model this aspect of the problem, we would need to go well beyond the full-information framework Kydland and Prescott used to deal with differently informed agents. Theorists have scarcely begun to explore *this* territory, and the examples that have been worked out are too stylized to give a clear idea of what sorts of dynamic possibilities they open up. But we are still talking about a real business cycle theory, in which monetary shocks play no role, and I do not see why such a theory would be expected to produce results that are terribly inconsistent with Kydland and Prescott's aggregative dynamics.

[97]

Now introducing money into this elaborated version of Kydland and Prescott's model, if it were done in the manner described for a much simpler system in the last section, would clearly introduce the inflation tax distortions from anticipated money movements, just as it does in simpler contexts. Whether *unanticipated* monetary shocks would induce additional real responses, over and above those due to their information effects, will depend on the nature of agents' information systems.

Surely agents will 'correct' for pure units changes that they can all observe and agree upon, whether they are interacting in a competitive way or via a system of contracts (written, presumably, contingent on relevant public information) or in some other way. Perhaps it would even be in the *collective* interest of all agents if all of them could agree to process sufficient information each period to do this, though this would obviously depend on the resource costs of doing so. But it seems to me most unlikely that it would be in the private interest of individual agents to specialize their individual information systems so as to be well-equipped to adapt for units changes of a purely monetary origin. In so far as they do not, equilibria in systems with private information ought to have monetary non-neutralities that do not have counterparts in full information systems.

My paper 'Expectations and the neutrality of money' gives a simple example in which this

[98]

conjecture can be verified.[5] In that example, producers are placed in a situation where the dollar expenditures on their output (ultimately, on their labor) fluctuate *relative to* expenditures on other producers' output, and preferences and technology are such that producers will respond to such shifts by varying their productive efforts. The economic logic of this response is exactly the same as the logic of producer responses to technology shifts in Kydland and Prescott. In my paper, however, *total* dollar expenditures also fluctuate due to fluctuations in the money supply, and producers are unable to distinguish, either through direct information or indirectly through the information conveyed by price movements, whether a particular demand shift is a relative shift (to which they would like to respond by producing more) or an aggregate shift (to which they would respond, if they could, with a monetary 'units' correction only). Two 'bits' of information are needed to make the right decision, but agents are assumed to have only one. As a result, agents react to monetary shocks that would be neutral in a full-information system as though they were real shocks: they behave as if they were subject to 'money illusion' (as in Modigliani's paper), or as if they had signed contracts agreeing to behave as though they had money illusion (as in Taylor's and Lucas's papers).

5 Lucas, 'Expectations and the neutrality of money'.

The example in my paper does not have very interesting dynamics, since in order to keep things analyzable, capital in all its forms was excluded from the model. Yet it does not seem to me at all implausible that in a model such as Kydland and Prescott's, elaborated so as to admit limited information on the part of agents, that shocks of monetary origin would be 'misread' by agents as signaling changes in technology or preferences, and hence trigger the same kind of dynamic response that technology shocks do in the model they reported.[6] Indeed, it is hard to imagine how it could be otherwise.

We do not, certainly, want to confuse conjectures about models no one can as yet write down

6 Robert E. Lucas, Jr, 'An equilibrium model of the business cycle', *Journal of Political Economy* **83** (1975), pp. 1113–44, is a kind of intermediate model to Lucas, 'Expectations and the neutrality of money'; and Kydland and Prescott. It provides some support for the opinion in the text.

More recent theoretical models, in which limited information and monetary shocks interact (in different ways) so as to give rise to real responses, include Sanford J. Grossman and Laurence Weiss, 'Heterogeneous information and the business cycle', *Journal of Political Economy* **90** (1982), pp. 699–727; and Sanford J. Grossman, Oliver D. Hart and Eric S. Maskin, 'Unemployment with observable aggregate shocks', *Journal of Political Economy* **91** (1983), pp. 907–27. A useful recent survey of these and other related theoretical developments is Jose A. Scheinkman, 'General Equilibrium Models of Economic Fluctuations: a survey of theory', unpublished University of Chicago working paper, 1984.

[100]

and solve with operational, simulatable systems like Kydland and Prescott's, and I do not want this discussion misinterpreted in this way. But a great deal of criticism that equilibrium models have received has taken the form of conjectures about phenomena that are thought to be paradoxical from the point of view of such models *as a class*. It has always surprised me that the class of equilibrium models was not instead subject to criticism on grounds of vacuity: there are just a lot of possibilities for dynamic systems with incomplete information. Thomas Sargent's paper, 'On the Observational Equivalence of Natural and Unnatural Theories of Macroeconomics' long ago demonstrated the subtlety, perhaps even the impossibility, of discriminating between the broad class of models in which monetary non-neutralities arise for informational reasons, and the class of models in which money affects real variables in some other way.[7]

7 Thomas J. Sargent, 'On the observational equivalence of natural and unnatural theories of macroeconomics', *Journal of Political Economy* **84** (1976), pp. 631–40. A great deal of recent empirical research (including some of my own) has focused on attempts to discriminate between broad *classes* of possible macroeconomic models (Keynesian, classical, and so on) without attempting to articulate any particular representative model of any of these classes. Such a strategy, if successful, would obviously be useful in narrowing the class of theoretical models one would want to concentrate on, but examples such as Sargent's, and a quite different one of Stokey's and mine ('Money and interest in a cash-in-

Economists since David Hume have suspected that the real consequences of monetary instability arise because people misread nominal signals as containing information they do not in fact have. It would seem a shame to back off from this ancient line of thought just as we are beginning to develop the tools to do something interesting with it.

---

advance economy' – see note 3 of section VI) make it clear, I think, that this strategy is largely futile. Attempts, like Kydland and Prescott's or John Taylor's or Thomas Sargent's (or, for that matter, the older Keynesian econometric models) to develop and test particular structural models seem less decisive (because one has no way of knowing whether their shortcomings are shortcomings of the class of models from which they are drawn or only of their particular structure) than reduced-form tests, but they are more useful, I think, in advancing the scientific discussion.

VIII

At the beginning of these lectures, I said that I thought the incorporation into macroeconomics of the methods of economic dynamics would lead to radical changes in the way we think about economic policy. Now that I have gone into some detail about these theoretical developments, I can be more specific about the nature of these changes, and this will be a good way to conclude my discussion.

First, and I think most fundamental, taking a dynamic point of view involves thinking of private agents as choosing contingency plans for the current and future variables under their control, taking as given their *expectations* about the way other economic actors are going to behave. Symmetrically, it follows that one cannot usefully think about economic policy – about the strategies of government, another 'player' in this game – in terms of current policy decisions only. Private agents necessarily have to make inferences about the way future fiscal and monetary policy will be conducted. If we discuss policy as though it involved only what government does today – that is, if we discuss policy in the terms that dominate current political discussion – then we are leaving the most important aspects of policy undiscussed and their consequences unanalyzed.

This observation is a commonplace from the point of view of the theory of dynamic games: one cannot even *state* a policy question in the language of section II without assenting to it. It also reflects a traditional view that long predates modern theoretical formulations, to the effect that the most useful way to think about government policy is as a choice of *rules of the game* to which government is committed for some length of time. This is why democratic governments have constitutions that are difficult to change and legal systems that respect precedents and 'due process'. So it is that quite recent developments in economic theory are reintroducing into macroeconomic policy discussions important considerations that were momentarily swept aside by the stresses of the Great Depression and by the intellectual response of Keynesianism. We need, in Buchanan and Wagner's useful terminology, an 'economic constitution' and we are at last beginning to develop the economic theory that will be helpful in designing it.[1]

1 James M. Buchanan and Richard E. Wagner, *Democracy in Deficit* (Academic Press, New York, 1977).

Second – and this point is almost as model-free as the first – the post-war business cycle is just not a very important problem in terms of individual welfare. The gains from removing *all* existing variability from aggregate consumption – even if this could be done with *no* evil side effects (which it could not) – are surely well below 1 per cent of national income. Policies that deal with the very real problems of society's less fortunate – wealth redistribution and social insurance – can be designed in total ignorance of the nature of business-cycle dynamics (as many such useful programs have been), and the discovery of better business cycle theories will contribute little or nothing to improved design. There is a real and dangerous hypocrisy involved in discussing unemployment rates of 10 per cent as though they raise a temporary problem that can be dealt with by fiscal deficits or monetary expansions. Unemployment in the USA is 7 per cent now at business-cycle *peaks*. This is not a problem of year-to-year fine tuning, and it does no service to unemployed people to talk about it as though it were.

A third conclusion can also be drawn without resolving any of the really hard problems of economic dynamics, though it is an application of the quantity theory of money. According to any coherent existing theory, and any theory I can see on the horizon, a society can use monetary and fiscal policy to attain any *average* inflation rate it wants. This conclusion has *nothing* to do with the responsiveness of monetary and fiscal decision variables to short-term fluctuations in the state of the economy. The only 'cruel choice' involved in the selection of the average rate of inflation has to do with the tax rates imposed on money-using activities – the 'inflation tax'. At inflation rates below 10 per cent, this is a minor issue (that is, it is of the same order of magnitude as the issue of the business fluctuations of the post-war period), but at higher rates the deadweight loss can be serious. Long-run price stability is one of the few legitimate 'free lunches' economics has discovered in 200 years of trying. It – and the interest rates of 3 per cent or so that come with it – can be had for the asking.

To go beyond these three observations to questions involving the efficiency of alternative kinds of stabilization policy involves moving to – or, I would say, beyond – the current frontiers of macroeconomics. If one accepts the model of Kydland and Prescott as a working approximation, economic fluctuations of the magnitude of the post-war period in the USA are interpreted as efficient resource allocations, as a best response to shocks originating in 'nature'. The conclusion is not that further consumption stabilization is impossible – this is surely *not* the case in the context of this model – but that it is undesirable, that consumption smoothing policies would induce inefficiencies that more than offset the benefits from reduced risk. Certainly no one would

[106]

argue that Kydland and Prescott's work has *established* this conclusion, but neither do I believe that it can be firmly rejected on the basis of currently available evidence.

If, on the other hand, one assigns a role to monetary instability as an independent cause of real fluctuations, due either to 'inflation tax' considerations or to some form of incompleteness of agents' information, efficiency gains are possible from policies that stabilize the fluctuations about trend in the supply of money. The calculations in section II provide a rough upper bound for these gains: they are not impressive. To determine what fraction of these gains could be achieved without inducing inefficient side-effects would require a model that is capable of partitioning observed consumption variability into the part that is due to 'technology' and the part due to monetary instability. I have sketched what seem to me to be the key ingredients of such a model in section VII, but as an operational, simulatable system, it does not yet exist.

The most interesting recent developments in macroeconomic theory seem to me describable as the reincorporation of aggregative problems such as inflation and the business cycle within the general framework of 'microeconomic' theory. If these developments succeed, the term 'macroeconomic' will simply disappear from use and the modifier 'micro' will become superfluous. We will simply speak, as did Smith, Ricardo, Marshall and

[107]

Walras, of *economic* theory. If we are honest, we will have to face the fact that at any given time there will be phenomena that are well-understood from the point of view of the economic theory we have, and other phenomena that are not. We will be tempted, I am sure, to relieve the discomfort induced by discrepancies between theory and facts by saying that the ill-understood facts are the province of some other, different kind of economic theory. Keynesian 'macroeconomics' was, I think, a surrender (under great duress) to this temptation. It led to the abandonment, for a class of problems of great importance, of the use of the only 'engine for the discovery of truth' that we have in economics. Now we are once again putting this engine of Marshall's to work on the problems of aggregate dynamics. There is much to be done, but there is an exciting sense of real progress in the enterprise, and I am full of hope.

Index

[109]

[113]